Implementing Lean Six Sigma throughout the Supply Chain

The Comprehensive and Transparent Case Study

Implementing Lean Six Sigma throughout the Supply Chain

The Comprehensive and Transparent Case Study

Elizabeth A. Cudney • Rodney Kestle

CRC Press
Taylor & Francis Group
Boca Raton London New York

CRC Press is an imprint of the
Taylor & Francis Group, an **informa** business

A PRODUCTIVITY PRESS BOOK

Productivity Press
Taylor & Francis Group
270 Madison Avenue
New York, NY 10016

© 2011 by Taylor and Francis Group, LLC
Productivity Press is an imprint of Taylor & Francis Group, an Informa business

No claim to original U.S. Government works

Printed in the United States of America on acid-free paper
10 9 8 7 6 5 4 3 2 1

International Standard Book Number: 978-1-4398-2814-4 (Paperback)

Library of Congress Cataloging-in-Publication Data

Cudney, Elizabeth A.
   Implementing lean six sigma throughout the supply chain : the comprehensive and transparent case study / Elizabeth A. Cudney, Rodney Kestle.
       p. cm.
     Includes index.
     ISBN 978-1-4398-2814-4 (pbk. : alk. paper)
     1. Six sigma (Quality control standard)--Case studies. 2. Business logistics--Quality control--Case studies. 3. Business logistics--Management--Case studies. I. Kestle, Rodney. II. Title.

HD38.5.C856 2011
658.7--dc22   2010034679

Visit the Taylor & Francis Web site at
http://www.taylorandfrancis.com

and the Productivity Press Web site at
http://www.productivitypress.com

Dedication

My greatest appreciation goes to my family for supporting me, believing in me, and their love. Without such appreciated support, fulfilling this dream would not have been possible. My husband, Brian, and our two wonderful children, Caroline and Josh, bring me the greatest joy.

Elizabeth A. Cudney

This book is dedicated to my wife Kimberly and children Isabella, Madeline, and Caroline. Thank you for your support and patience and for inspiring me to reach further.

Rodney Kestle

Contents

Acknowledgments

We are indebted to the colleagues who we have had the fortune to work with and learn from. They have challenged our thinking and showed us what Lean Six Sigma is truly about.

We are extremely thankful to the Productivity Press for all their help and for making this a remarkable experience for us. In particular, we would like to thank Michael Sinocchi, senior acquisitions editor, and Lara Zoble, assistant editor and project coordinator. We are also grateful to Prudence Board, project editor, for her development edits.

Authors

Elizabeth Cudney, PhD, is an assistant professor at Missouri University of Science and Technology in the Engineering Management and Systems Engineering Department. She received her B.S. in industrial engineering from North Carolina State University, her Master of Engineering in mechanical engineering with a manufacturing specialization and Master of Business Administration from the University of Hartford; and she received her doctorate in engineering management from the University of Missouri–Rolla.

Prior to returning to school for her doctorate, she worked for seven years in the automotive industry in various roles including Six Sigma Black Belt, quality/process engineer, quality auditor, senior manufacturing engineer, and manufacturing manager. In 2010, Beth was inducted into the International Academy for Quality. Beth received the 2007 ASQ A. V. Feigenbaum Medal and the 2006 SME Outstanding Young Manufacturing Engineering Award. Beth is an ASQ-certified Six Sigma Black Belt, certified quality engineer, manager of quality/operational excellence, certified quality inspector, certified quality improvement associate, certified quality technician, and certified quality process analyst. Beth is currently faculty advisor for the ASEM/IIE student chapter at Missouri University of Science and Technology. Beth cochaired the 2009 IIE Operational Excellence Conference. She served as cochair of the 2008 IIE Operational Excellence Conference and cochair of the 2007 IIE/ASQ Lean and Quality Conference. Beth also served as cochair of the 2006 IIE/ASQ Quality Drives Lean Conference and cochair of the 2004 and 2005 IIE Lean Management Solutions Conferences. She served on the conference committee for the 2008, 2009, and IIE Annual Conferences. Beth also recently completed a two-year term as the president of the IIE Lean Division. She is president of the Rotary Club of Rolla, Missouri. Beth is a member of the American Society of Engineering Management (ASEM), American Society of Mechanical Engineers (ASME), American Society for Quality (ASQ), Institute of Industrial Engineers (IIE), and Society of Automotive Engineers (SAE). Beth's major areas of interest are in quality engineering and Lean enterprise, more specifically Mahalanobis-Taguchi System, robust design, Lean enterprise, and Six Sigma. She currently teaches EMgt 266 Quality Philosophies and Methods, EMgt 309 Six Sigma, and EMgt 409 Design for Six Sigma. Beth has published more than 50 papers, 11 journal papers, and has four additional journal papers waiting for publication. In addition, her first book, *Using Hoshin Kanri to Improve the Value Stream*, was released in March 2009 through Productivity Press, a division of Taylor and Francis.

Rodney Kestle completed his BS degree at Purdue University's School of Technology in 1997. While a student at Purdue University, he completed internships with Modine Manufacturing and Honeywell. After graduation in 1997, he took a position with the Intel Corporation as a manufacturing equipment technician at their Chandler, Arizona facility. There he became the equipment owner for the metrology tools, which made him responsible for the maintenance user specifications and the training of other equipment technicians for this tool set. In July 1998, he left Intel and took a position as an industrial engineer at Thomas Engineering Inc., located in Hoffman Estates, Illinois. During the next six and a half years, Rodney became an expert on tablet tooling manufacturing and design. Early in his stay, he took on the responsibility as Thomas Engineering's quality manager and implemented their first formal quality system for all divisions of the company. In January 2005, Rodney joined Brown and Sharpe as an applications engineer for coordinate measuring machines (CMM). While at their Elgin, Illinois office, he spent most of his time in the classroom teaching their customers about the use and operation of CMMs and the PC-based software that operated the equipment. This class time motivated him to return to school to further his education, with the goal being a PhD.

In August 2006, Rodney began his course work at Missouri University of Science and Technology under the School of Engineering's Manufacturing Engineering Masters program. With the completion of his thesis, he was granted a Master of Science in manufacturing engineering in December 2008. Rodney is now pursuing his doctorate in engineering management at Missouri University of Science and Technology.

Chapter 1

Introduction

Real-world examples and hands-on experience are invaluable resources when instructing the use of methods and tools in training or in a classroom. However, instructors may not have access to these resources, and thus they can teach only theory and basic examples. Another solution is the use of case studies in the teaching process. Case studies can enhance the learning experience by giving the learner a role in a real scenario. The story of the case study adds life to a seemingly lifeless group of tools. From this perspective, Six Sigma and Lean methods taught with the aid of case studies may help some novices to better assimilate the tools, since they are presented as a whole.

The primary objective of this book is to provide a Lean Six Sigma case study following the Define–Measure–Analyze–Improve–Control (DMAIC) process that is used in the retail industry. The purpose is to facilitate Lean Six Sigma instruction by providing an interactive case study. The case study will enable the learners to apply the DMAIC phases by providing data and information on a distribution center.

This book provides a comprehensive Lean Six Sigma case study from start to finish. The book follows a team as they implement a Lean Six Sigma project. What is unique about this book is that it presents all the necessary information to clearly show how and why the team made the decisions they made. Current published case studies are very brief and only give a high-level overview of what the team did. This in-depth case study presents all of the data used by the team, which is also given in the CD that accompanies this book, and comprehensively explains how the team drew their conclusions. Thus the reader can use the data to make the same analyses and conclusions. There is a clear linkage between all of the Lean Six Sigma tools that provides numerous threads from all the necessary tools.

How To Use the CD

Throughout the book, numerous graphs and charts are presented, and data analysis is provided. The data for these charts and graphs can be found on the CD included at the back of the book. These data sets are designed to help you plan and execute your Lean Six Sigma journey. In addition, a series of presentation slides are provided to supplement the instruction of the case study. The following section describes the CD contents and user information. We hope you find the data sets, training slides, and tools useful in your Lean Six Sigma deployment.

CD Instructions

The CD that accompanies this book contains several files that include data sets, training slides, and tools for your Lean Six Sigma journey.

The CD files are:

- *Data sets* (Excel files): Each data set is named to correspond with a Figure or Table in the book. For example, the data for Figure 4.4 is named "Data Figure 4.4."
- *Training slides* (PowerPoint files): These files correspond to the DMAIC methodology used throughout the book. All figures that are used in the book are included in these files to provide training documents to teach the case.
- *Glossary*: This file is a reference guide that also appears at the end of the book and contains commonly used Six Sigma and Lean definitions.

We hope you enjoy your journey to becoming a Lean Six Sigma organization!

Chapter 2

Lean Six Sigma Overview

Lean and Six Sigma (6σ) are powerful philosophies backed by several tools for improving quality, productivity, profitability, and market competitiveness for any corporation. Lean philosophies focus on eliminating waste and improving flow using various proven methods initially pioneered by the Toyota Manufacturing Company under the banner of the Toyota Production System (TPS). Six Sigma is focused on reducing process variation using problem-solving and statistical tools. It was first perfected by the Motorola Company and most notably deployed by Jack Welch during his tenure as CEO of General Electric (GE). Both methods, when used independently, can produce positive results for the user, but when applied in a holistic manner, they complement each other well and provide more dramatic gains.

Again, Lean emphasizes the elimination of waste and creation of flow within an enterprise. Lean's primary focus is on the customer, to address value-added (VA) and non-value-added (NVA) tasks. Value-added tasks are the only operations for which the customer is ready or willing to pay. Typically, these are processes that transform the product or service based on customer requirements. The idea of creating flow in Lean is to deliver products and services just in time (JIT), in the right amounts, and at the right quality levels at the right place. This necessitates that products and services be produced and delivered only when a pull is exerted by the customer through a signal in the form of a purchase. A well-designed Lean system allows for an immediate and effective response to fluctuating customer demands and requirements. Lean tools that are most commonly used to eliminate waste and achieve flow are value-stream mapping (VSM), standard work, 5S (sort, set in order, shine, standardize, sustain), single-minute exchange of dies (SMED), and visual management.

Like Lean, Six Sigma is also a customer-focused improvement strategy. At the core of the method, Six Sigma utilizes a discipline that strives to minimize defects and variation of critical variables toward an achievement of 3.4 defects per million opportunities in product design, production, and administrative processes. Customer satisfaction and cost reduction can be realized by reducing variation in processes that produce the products and services that they use. While focused on reducing variation, the Six Sigma methodology uses a well-defined problem-solving approach with the application of statistical tools. The methodology uses five phases: Define–Measure–Analyze–Improve–Control (DMAIC). The purpose of the five phases is to define the problem, measure the process performance, analyze the process for root causes, improve the process by eliminating or reducing root causes, and control the improved process to hold the gains.

The goals of Six Sigma include developing a world-class culture, developing leaders, and supporting long-range objectives. There are numerous benefits of Six Sigma, including a stronger knowledge of products and processes, a reduction in defects, an increased customer satisfaction level that generates business growth and improves profitability, an increase in communication and teamwork, and a common set of tools.

Six Sigma is commonly credited to Bill Smith, an engineer at Motorola, who coined the term in 1984. The concept was originally developed as a safety margin of 50% in design for product-performance specifications. This safety margin was equivalent to a Six Sigma level of capability. Since its first introduction, Six Sigma has continued to evolve over time and has been adopted throughout the world as a standard business practice.

When Lean or Six Sigma is deployed independently, only a few companies have shown strong improvements. This book demonstrates a synergistic merger of the tools in a Lean Six Sigma case study to be used for training or course instruction. By using the Six Sigma tool of DMAIC, the two methods can be merged based on the time of implementation. An integrated approach to process improvement using Lean and Six Sigma principles is required, since both Lean and Six Sigma represent more of a cultural change in the way that a company does business rather than one-time tools to be used for quick improvement. Without a model to allow merging of the tools, the proper understanding of the tools may be lost.

The case study presented in this book was developed from a composite of experiences, and it centers on a fictitious company called "CJMart," which is a global retail store with numerous distribution centers. The case study has been constructed to focus on a breakthrough

Define	Measure	Analyze	Improve	Control
• Project Charter	• Process Map	• Cause & Effect	• Quality Function Deployment	• Control Plan
• Stakeholder Analysis	• Voice of Customer (VOC)	• Diagram	• Action Plan	• <u>Mistake Proofing</u>
• Supplier-Input-Process-Output-Customer (SIPOC)	• Data Collection Plan	• 5 Whys	• Cost/Benefit Analysis	• <u>Standard Work</u>
	• Pareto Chart	• Test for Normality	• Future State Map	• FMEA
• Project Plan	• Histogram	• Failure Modes and Effects Analysis (FMEA)	• Design of Experiments	• Training Plan
• Responsibilities Matrix	• Scatter Diagram		• Main Effects and Interaction Plots	• Process Capability
• Ground Rules	• Process Capability	• Correlation Analysis		• Statistical Process Control (SPC)
• Critical-to-Satisfaction (CTS) Tree	• Process Statistics	• Regression Analysis	• <u>Dashboards/ Scorecards</u>	• Standard Operating Procedures (SOP)
	• Benchmarking	• Hypothesis Tests		• Lessons Learned
	• Gauge R&R	• <u>8 Wastes</u>		
	• Cost of Poor Quality	• <u>5S</u>		
	• <u>Current State Map</u>	• <u>Kaizen</u>		

Figure 2.1   Lean Six Sigma DMAIC process and tools.

in trailer utilization for a distribution center. Trailer utilization is a metric used by supply-chain management to monitor the efficiency of trailer use. The case study begins with an introduction of the company and its need for the breakthrough. The book then steps through the Six Sigma phases of Define–Measure–Analyze–Improve–Control to illustrate how a team implemented Lean Six Sigma. The timing of the integration of Lean tools within the DMAIC process is important. Figure 2.1 shows the Lean Six Sigma DMAIC phases and the respective tools. The Lean tools are shown with an underline.

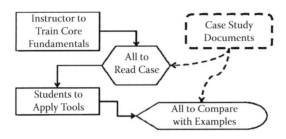

Figure 2.2   Flow of the desired instruction process.

For those using this as a textbook for training, the purpose of the case was to support the instruction of Lean Six Sigma fundamentals. Figure 2.2 shows the flow of the desired instruction process, where the case study is defined as two separate modules: the case information and completed tools. By the nature of the flow, the case information contains enough facts and data to allow a learner to use the tools in an applied exercise before examining the completed tools.

The case study story is told sequentially to demonstrate when each tool is to be used. Some of the tools could be completed concurrently, but for ease of instruction, the case study is presented as a series of actions. Once each tool is understood, it will become clear to the reader that some tools and activities do not rely on another's completion. Writing the case study in series also helps foster the creation of exercises for the reader to practice the tools via the data that is provided. Note that the case uses as many tools as possible for the sake of demonstrating their use in a learning environment. Typically, a Lean Six Sigma project only uses the tools necessary to gain a breakthrough, thus minimizing the time to complete the project.

Chapter 3

Case Study Introduction

CJMart is a U.S.-based global distribution company. After the most recent board meeting, the CEO revealed the company strategy for the coming year. To help meet shareholders' demands and reduce costs, the CEO declared that the company must reduce operating costs by 15% to ensure the increase of annual profits by 10%. Though this task was spread across the entire company, the senior vice president (SVP) of logistics aligned all teams and challenged them to develop a list of projects along with financial savings and resource requirements tied to each. Once this task was completed, the various departments presented their findings to the Logistics Executive Team (see Figure 3.1 for organizational chart). After many hours of negotiation, the team was able to jointly set an achievable objective to reduce their internal operating costs by 10%. This cost reduction goal was spread throughout all logistics regions and to the local operating staff.

Joe Thompson, Midwest distribution vice president (VP), and Anita Smith, Midwest transportation VP, both received an e-mail requesting an agreement to reduce

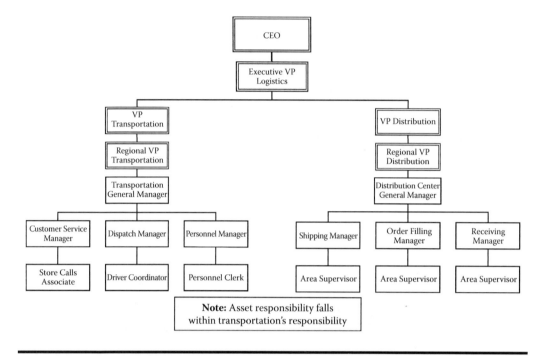

Figure 3.1 Organizational chart.

their operating costs by 3.6%. Due to the large volume of their business, the 3.6% reduction translates to over $300 million in annual savings. Joe and Anita knew that reducing operating costs on that scale would mean reexamining their entire logistics process. Joe and Anita joined forces and held an emergency meeting with their local operators.

Anita proudly stated, "This is a goal that needs some breakthrough thinking! To meet the goal of a 3.6% reduction in operating costs, we need to apply a different thought process and work together for a solution." Anita Smith had recently completed Lean Six Sigma training at CJMart and recommended applying the Lean Six Sigma methodology to identify areas of improvement and leverage the local operators to drive process improvement. Anita is very knowledgeable of the subject, but not quite an expert. Her experience of 17 years in retail and distribution will be an asset to the project.

Joe mentioned, "We need to assemble a team with the help of an expert in Lean Six Sigma." From there, Joe and Anita knew what to do. Joe formulated a reply to the Logistics Executive Team's e-mail stating that he and Ms. Smith would take the challenge of reducing their operating costs, but that they would need a Lean Six Sigma specialist to help direct their efforts. Jim Pulls, a Master Black Belt (MBB), was then assigned to help all logistics regions throughout the country with their cost-reduction goals.

Back in the Midwest, a core team was being formed, which included Joe, Anita, and Jim. They met and discussed the list of opportunities developed by the logistics engineering teams and identified which ideas to apply to their business region. They agreed that driving utility into their trailer equipment could be a quick way to impact the bottom line. In order to drive utility into the equipment, they must reduce the number of days that trailers sit idle at distribution centers, behind stores, and at vendors, and increase the number of turns of trailers in transit between locations. The team agreed that the measure of a trailer's utility would be defined as trailer utilization (what percentage of time a trailer is in use versus sitting idle). Therefore, to improve it, they would need up-to-date trailer status data that would feed into an optimized dispatch plan. The following is a summary of the case.

- CEO requests 15% reduction of operating costs for company.
- This translates to a 10% reduction of operating costs for the Logistics division.

- The Midwest region of Logistics is requested to reduce operating costs by 3.6% to meet CEO's requests.
- Midwest region forms a Lean Six Sigma team.
- Lean Six Sigma team chooses trailer utilization as the process to be improved with a goal of cost reduction.

The Lean Six Sigma team now had an objective: to investigate and identify changes in trailer utilization that would result in a 3.6% reduction of the Midwest logistics operating costs within a 4–6 month time period. As another requirement, a final report to the SVP of logistics should summarize all of the options available, the potential savings for each option, and supporting evidence based on the Lean Six Sigma analysis process. During the investigation, the Lean Six Sigma team will have access to any member within the transportation and distribution groups. The access will be arranged ahead of time and will be conducted in a professional and unobtrusive manner. The goal is to help the Midwest logistics group meet the company's strategic goals.

Now that the project and goals have been selected, the team moves forward with following the DMAIC methodology to improve trailer utilization. In the next chapter, the team begins the Define phase to identify the customers for the process and their requirements.

Chapter 4

Define Phase

Introduction

While in the Define phase, the Lean Six Sigma team needs to establish the cause of their problem and set the boundaries of the problem. The team should use the Define phase to picture the process over time and provide insight about where the focus of improvement efforts should be. In this case, we already know that the improvement should be about trailer utilization, but what are the other factors that relate to trailer utilization? During the Define phase, it is critical to define who the customers are, what their requirements for trailer utilization are, and what their expectations are. These requirements and expectations are also known as the critical-to-satisfaction (CTS) characteristics. By using a high-level process map, the Supplier–Input–Process–Output–Customer (SIPOC) diagram, they will also define the project's boundaries, the process(es) to improve, and what to improve. So, let's get back to the case.

As Anita and Jim begin the project, they start by meeting with Senior Dispatch Manager Robert Quincy, Sr.

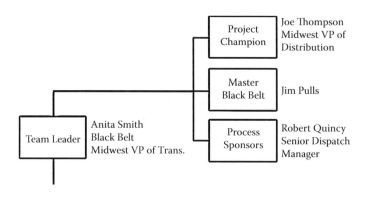

Figure 4.1   Core project team organization.

Robert oversees all dispatch operations for the entire Midwest region. Anita and Jim understand the importance of gaining the support of the process sponsor. Therefore, they meet with Robert to explain the project and its importance to the company as a whole. Robert agrees to help the team with access to the processes and his employees. Now, with the addition of the process sponsor, the core team is complete (see Figure 4.1).

Midwest Logistics, Lean Six Sigma Core Team

Project champion: Joe Thompson, Midwest VP of distribution

Master Black Belt: Jim Pulls

Process sponsor: Robert Quincy, senior dispatch manager

Team leader: Anita Smith, Midwest VP of transportation (Black Belt)

With the core project team identified, the group developed a responsibility matrix (RASIC) to identify the responsible (R), approval (A), support (S), inform (I), and consult (C) roles for each team member to ensure that they understood their role(s) and responsibilities. The RASIC matrix is shown in Figure 4.2.

With the roles defined for the team, it was now time for the team to ask some critical questions to lay the framework of the project. These questions would help solidify the need, goals, deliverables, and deadlines for the project and get the entire team moving in the same direction. These questions included:

- Why must this project be done now?
- What is the business case of this project?
- Who is the customer?
- What is the current state?
- What will be the future state?
- What is the scope of the project?
- What are the tangible deliverables?
- What is the due date?

Using this information, the team formed a high-level process-improvement statement, as shown in Figure 4.3, to get the core team focusing on the same goal.

Joe Thompson, the project champion, began the next meeting by restating the immediate need for this project. Joe explained to the team that, with the decreasing demand and increased competition, it was necessary for the company to reduce operating costs by 15% for the overall company. The Logistics division had agreed to reduce their operating costs by 10%, which trickled down to a 3.6% reduction in operating costs for the Midwest region based on historical data as a baseline. The breakdown by region is given in Figure 4.4 (Data Figure 4.4).

With decreasing demand, customers were also hit hard, so product sales prices needed to be lowered to

Responsible (R) Approval (A) Support (S) Inform (I) Consult (C)	Team Leader Anita Smith	Process Owner Robert Quincy	Project Champion Joe Thompson	CI Mentor/MBB Jim Pulls	Finance Joe Thompson
Develop Initial Documents					
Form Core Team	R	I	A	A	C
Define Activities and Deliverables for Define Phase	R	I	A	A	I
Responsibility Matrix	R	I	A	C	I
Project Charter	R	S	A	C	S
SIPOC	R	S	A	C	I
Identify Stakeholders & Communication Plan					
Stakeholder Analysis Matrix	R	S	A	C	S
TPC Analysis	R	S	A	C	S
Customers/Stakeholders Matrix	R	S	A	C	S
Communication Plan	R	S	A	C	S
Perform Initial VOC and Identify CTS					
CTS Summary	R	S	A	C	S
Select Team and Launch the Project					
Team Organization Chart	R	S	A	C	S
Revise Responsibility Matrix	R	I	A	C	I
Items for Resolution (IFR) Form	R	S	A	C	S
Establish Ground Rules	R	S	A	C	S
Create Project Plan					
Macro Project Plan	R	S	A	C	S

Figure 4.2   RASIC matrix.

Process Improvement Statement

• The Logistics Midwest Region
  Lean Six-Sigma team will work
  on improving the utilization of
  trailers within the region.

• The basic process for trailer
  utilization is the same no
  matter who ships or receives.

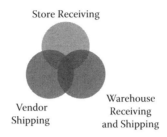

Figure 4.3   Process improvement statement.

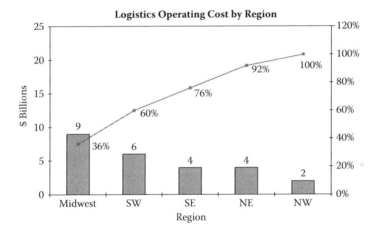

Figure 4.4   Logistics operating cost by region.

meet demand. Therefore, logistics operating costs needed
to be significantly reduced to aid in this effort.

Develop Initial Documents

Now that the team had agreed on the business case, Anita
organized a team meeting to develop the activities and
deliverables for the Define phase. The team determined
five major activities, which are shown in Figure 4.5.

Define Activities		Deliverables
1	Develop Initial Documents	1) Define Activities and Deliverables for Define Phase
		2) Core Team Responsibility Matrix
		3) Project Charter
		4) SIPOC
2	Identify Stakeholders and Communications Plan	5) Stakeholder Analysis Matrix
		6) TPC Analysis
		7) Customers/Stakeholders Matrix
		8) Communication Plan
3	Perform Initial VOC and Identify CTS	9) CTS Summary
4	Select Team and Launch the Project	10) Full Team Organization Chart
		11) Full Team Responsibilities Matrix
		a) IFR (Items for Resolution)
		b) Establish Ground Rules
5	Create Project Plan	12) Work plan

Figure 4.5 **Define activities and deliverables.**

Project Charter

The first major deliverable that needed a team discussion was the project charter. Anita called a meeting to develop the project charter where she noted that, in the Midwest region, trailer utilization accounts for 35% of the $9-billion operating budget. The costs associated with trailer utilization not only include transporting the trailer, but also its maintenance, storage, and replacement. Along with recordable accounting costs, the team

Account Name	Detail Cost	% of Cost	Annual Expense (millions)
Transportation Cost	Driver	17	$535.5
	Tractor Use	45	$1,417.5
	Fuel (for refrigeration)	13	$409.5
Maintenance Cost	Preventive Maintenance	2	$63
	Repairs	4	$126
	Insurance & License	1	$31.5
	Replacement	15	$472.5
Storage Cost	Land Rental	2	$63
	Security	1	$31.5

Figure 4.6   Trailer utilization cost breakout.

must realize the opportunity cost of being ready to meet peak shipping demand. So, to meet the cost-reduction goal of 3.6% ($324 million), the team needs to reduce the trailer utilization costs by 10.3%. The details of trailer utilization costs are outlined in Figure 4.6 (Data Figure 4.6). Jim Pulls reminded the team not to forget about documenting the impact and the consequences of staying in the current state.

Once the problem statement had been covered, a discussion of the project's scope was then started, again led by Anita. The team agreed quickly that the scope only includes the Midwest region, since this is their direct task. After considerable discussion, the team also determined that the scope includes (a) examining and recommending changes to the major process steps for use of a trailer, (b) limiting the investigation to only two methods of trailer unloading (live unload and drop and hook), and (c) deciding that unloading may occur at a distribution center or store.

The next step of developing the charter was to determine the customers/stakeholders and their critical-to-success factors. For this discussion, Anita asked Jim Pulls to help move the team in the right direction. An initial brainstorming list of the customers/stakeholders included:

- Driver
- Transportation personnel
- Warehouse receiving and shipping personnel
- Store receiving personnel
- Vendor shipping personnel

Now that the customers/stakeholders had been identified, a very lengthy discussion was held to develop an initial list of factors that are critical to success. These factors include:

1. Up-to-date trailer status
2. Optimized trailer dispatch plan
3. Open communication of critical or jeopardy events
4. Realistic process time estimates

The project goal, the scope, and the financial benefit of the project had been determined in previous meetings, so Anita restated each item and asked for final approval from the team. The team then finalized the project charter, as shown in Figure 4.7, and submitted it to the senior vice president (SVP) for management approval and signatures. This ensures that the team has complete support from top management. Then Jim Pulls asked the team about risk management for the project.

Project Name: Trailer Utilization Optimization

Project Overview:

In alignment with the company's strategic goals, the Logistics Executive team has jointly set the objective to reduce internal operating costs by 10%. This has translated to a 3.6% reduction of operating costs in the Midwest Logistics Region. The Midwest Logistics Region's Lean Six Sigma team has examined multiple projects that may impact the breakthrough goal and has identified optimizing trailer utilization as a high priority.

Problem Statement:

The Midwest Logistics Region needs to reduce operating costs by 3.6% ($324 million). Improving trailer utilization has been identified as the quickest way to reduce costs within their direct control. The Lean Six Sigma team needs to analyze the current state of trailer utilization, and then suggest improvements based on an optimized process within 4-6 months.

If the Midwest Logistics Region fails to show an opportunity to reduce operating costs as directed by the company's strategic plans within 4-6 months, the region would have to reduce operating costs by other means, such as labor cutbacks, procurement freezes, and contract renegotiations. By staying in the current state, the Midwest Logistics Region would have to choose unfavorable cost cutting methods which typically impact the productivity of the operation and may not meet the $324 million goal. If productivity is lost, shipments may not make it to the market on-time, thus reducing the total sales of the company. The final impact would be a devaluation of CJMart's stock due to its inability to meet the 10% profit increase projection.

Customer/Stakeholders:

Transportation Personnel, Warehouse Receiving Personnel, Warehouse Shipping Personnel, Drivers, Store Receiving Personnel, Vendor Shipping Personnel

What is important to these customers – CTS: Up-to-date trailer status, optimized trailer dispatch plan, open communication of critical or jeopardy events, and realistic process time estimates

Figure 4.7   Project charter.

Goal of the Project:

Reduce trailer utilization costs by 10.3%

Scope Statement:

The project is limited to the Midwest region for which Anita Smith and Joe Thompson are responsible. The Lean Six Sigma team will examine and recommend changes to the major process steps for the use of a trailer: dispatch, load, transport, dispatch update, and unload. The investigation is limited to the two methods of trailer use: live load/unload and drop'n hook. These methods of use may occur at a vendor, distribution center, or store.

Projected Financial Benefit(s):

Based on an operating budget of $9 billion, this project will attempt to avoid costs connected with trailer use in the Midwest region. The avoidance target is $324 million.

Figure 4.7   (continued).

Jim advised the team to manage risk by anticipating problems. Planning for problems is the best way to reduce or even avoid them. Even at this early point of the project, many risk events can be defined, and strategies to respond to them can be planned. Anita finalized the team charter by adding potential risks and project milestones, as shown in Figure 4.8. She ended the meeting by scheduling the next team meeting to develop SIPOC diagrams.

(Meeting side notes): Robert Quincy suggested the team make an assumption on the partnership between transportation, warehouse, store, and vendor personnel. He stated that the overall success of the project would depend heavily on these areas working closely together. Anita stressed the need for a complete process map to gather and analyze the process. She also felt strongly

Project Charter

Potential Risks	Probability of Risk (H/M/L)	Impact of Risk (H/M/L)	**Risk Mitigation Strategy**
Lack of Support	M	H	**Build Communication Plan**
Data not Available	L	H	**Retain Risk**
Resistance to Change from Transportation Office	M	H	**Include in Change Strategy**

Project Resources:

Team Leader: Anita Smith

Division and Dept.: Midwest Logistics Region

Process Owner: Robert Quincy, Sr. Dispatch Manager

Project Champion: Joe Thompson

Continuous Improvement Mentor/MBB: Jim Pulls

Finance: Joe Thompson

Team Members/Support Resources: Midwest Transportation Office

Milestones

Phase	Est. Completion Date
Define	2/2
Measure	3/2
Analyze	4/6
Improve	4/15
Control	4/27
Seek Approval	5/5

Figure 4.8   Potential risks and project milestones.

that this would provide a strong foundation of process knowledge for the team to move forward and make the right decisions for improvement.

Supplier–Input–Process–Output–Customer (SIPOC)

The team met again to develop the necessary SIPOC diagrams for the processes under consideration. The team listed numerous process steps:

1. Dispatch plan made for the day of operation.
2. Call made to driver.
3. Dispatch trailer to shipping dock.
4. Driver signs out a tractor.
5. Driver hooks up trailer and moves it to shipping dock.
6. Driver confirms location of trailer with shipping personnel.

7. Load product on trailer.
8. Driver picks up paperwork and secures load.
9. Transport trailer to store staging zone.
10. Driver reports status to transportation coordinator via cell phone.
11. Driver receives dispatch update.
12. Trailer arrives at receiving dock.
13. Driver presents paperwork to receiving dock (either waits for unload or drops off trailer).
14. Product unloaded.
15. Trailer dispatched to another shipping dock (this could be at a vendor or at a warehouse).

The team noted that this process is from warehouse to store. This could have been from vendor to warehouse as well. Figure 4.9 shows the possible routes that a trailer could travel during its use. The initial list of steps was reduced to include only those deemed critical by the team based on discussions with Robert, the process owner. For each of the critical process steps, the team developed an individual SIPOC, as shown in Figure 4.10. Customer requirements were typically to arrive on time and leave on time.

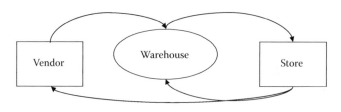

Figure 4.9   Trailer transportation routes.

Suppliers	Inputs	Processes	Outputs	Customers	
(Providers of the required resources)	(Resources required by the process)	(Top level description of the activity)	(Deliverables from the process)	(Anyone who receives a deliverable from the process)	
		Requirements		*Requirements*	
Driver Coord.	Dispatch Plan, Phone, Tractor, Trailer, Driver	Dispatch to Shipping Dock	Dock Location, Final Destination, Trailer at Dock	Arrive On Schedule (AOS)	Shipping Personnel
Shipping Personnel	Packing List, Product	Load Product	Trailer Ready to Transport	Leave On Schedule (LOS)	Driver
Driver	Travel Plan, Tractor, Trailer	Transport Trailer	Trailer Within Staging Zone	AOS	Driver Coord.
		Travel Within Legal Limits			
Driver	Cell Phone	Driver Reports Status	Verbal Communication	30 Minutes Before Arriving at Receiving Dock	Driver Coord.
Driver Coord.	Dispatch Plan, Phone	Driver Receives Dispatch Update	Rec. Dock Location, Trailer Status, Next Assignment	10 Minutes Before Arriving at Receiving Dock	Driver
Driver	Travel Plan, Tractor, Trailer	Arrives at Receiving Dock	Trailer Ready to Unload	AOS	Receiving Personnel
Receiving Personnel		Product Unload	Empty Trailer, Product, Trailer Status Update	LOS	Driver, W'house/Store, Driver Coord.

Figure 4.10 SIPOC.

Identify Stakeholders and Develop Communication Plan

In the next step, Anita led the team in identifying the stakeholders and developing a communication plan. The team decided to start by developing a stakeholder analysis matrix to address the potential impact or concerns of the stakeholders. The team broke down the stakeholders that were outlined in the project charter as follows:

- Transportation personnel
  General manager
  Dispatch manager
  Driver coordinator
- Driver (any driver of a CJMart trailer)
- Warehouse and receiving/shipping personnel
  Warehouse manager
  Receiving manager
  Shipping manager
  Dock personnel
- Vendor and shipping personnel
  Operations manager
  Shipping manager
  Dock personnel
- Store receiving personnel
  Store manager
  Receiving-dock personnel

Robert Quincy made sure the team noted that, within a region, there were multiple transportation offices and warehouses. Therefore, the stakeholder analysis and communication plan must be a generalization of the positions referenced.

Once the stakeholder analysis matrix was completed, as shown in Figure 4.11, the team began to look at the sources of resistance that would make change difficult within the project scope. The team performed a TPC analysis (Technical, Political, or Cultural) for each stakeholder group to figure out how to influence change. Again, the stakeholders were generalizations of the populations that each represented. The team also agreed to do a TPC analysis for a single person if any individuals were found to show more resistance than anticipated. Some of the examples of resistance for each stakeholder that the team brainstormed are listed here:

Transportation personnel
- Learn a new dispatch planning and execution process
- Why fix what isn't broke
- Lean Six Sigma team doesn't know my process

Driver (any driver of a CJMart trailer)
- Doesn't want to be watched so closely
- Thinks the schedule may become too rigid
- Doesn't want performance data tied to merit increases

Warehouse and receiving/shipping personnel
- Forced to work faster loading or unloading; may be unsafe and reduce quality
- Reduced number of personnel per load or unload event
- Not happy to have transportation pushing warehouse personnel

	Stakeholders	Who Are They?	Potential Impact or Concerns	
PRIMARY	Transportation Personnel	This includes the general manager, dispatch manager, and driver coordinators for each transportation office in the Midwest region.	• Manage optimized plan	+
			• Clear and timely communication	+
			• Able to adapt to changing conditions effecting plan	−
	Driver	This includes any driver moving a CJ-Mart owned trailer.	• Must champion optimized plan	+
			• First point of contact in field	−
			• Clear and timely communication	−
	Warehouse Receiving/Shipping Personnel	This includes the warehouse manager, the receiving manager, and the shipping manager. It also includes dock personnel that load and unload the trailer.	• Indirect link	−
			• Must know goal of optimized pian	−
			• Must have buy in	−
	Vendor Shipping Personnel	This includes the operations manager, shipping manager, and the dock personnel.	• Indirect link	−
			• Must know goal of optimized plan	−
			• Must have buy in	−
	Store Receiving Personnel	This includes the store manager and receiving dock personnel.	• Indirect link	−
			• Must know goal of optimized plan	−
			• Must have buy in	−
			• Needs goods	+

Figure 4.11   Stakeholder analysis.

Vendor and shipping personnel
  ■ Worried that trailers will be taken at unpredictable or inconsistent times
Store receiving personnel
  ■ Afraid new standards will be set for unloading trailers that are too difficult and dangerous

This enabled Anita to help the team understand the nature of the resistance they may face with implementing the project. The team also assigned percentages for the resistance based on whether they felt it would be technical, political, or cultural. In addition, this helped the team identify strategies and apply influence pressure to overcome resistance.

The team then brainstormed the sources of resistance and completed the TPC analysis for each stakeholder to ensure that all impacts and concerns were identified and addressed, as shown in Figures 4.12–4.16.

Next, the team used the information from the TPC analysis to build a customer/stakeholders matrix, as shown in Figures 4.17–4.20. Then, based on the gap between the stakeholder's current and future position, the team drafted a communication/influence strategy and assigned a strategy manager. For each of the stakeholders, Anita led the team in identifying the potential level of resistance and then developed a communication strategy to mitigate the resistance, preferably before it could even occur. Based on the current level of resistance, the team brainstormed possible communication strategies and then used a team vote to decide the strategies that would be used. The matrices identified strategy

Transportation Personnel			
Source of resistance	*Define causes of resistance*	*Examples from our project*	*Rating*
Technical	**Aligning and structuring organization** • Habit and inertia • Difficulty in learning new skills • Sunk costs • Lack of skills	• Learn a new dispatch planning and execution process	20
Political	**Allocating power and resources** • Threat to the old guard from the new guard • Relationships • Power and authority imbalance or self-preservation	• Lean Six Sigma team doesn't know my business.	40
Cultural	**Articulating the glue or cultural norms** • Selective perception • Locked into old "mindset" • Afraid of letting go	• Why fix what works?	40

Figure 4.12   TPC analysis for transportation personnel.

managers as team members that would be joining the team soon (added later, as shown in Figure 4.27).

Communications Strategy List

Based on the customer/stakeholder matrices developed by the team and the communication strategies selected, the team then brainstormed various methods of communication. Anita listed potential methods for communication as:

■ Weekly meetings
■ Monthly meetings

Driver			
Source of resistance	*Define causes of resistance*	*Examples from our project*	*Rating*
Technical	**Aligning and structuring organization** • Habit and inertia • Difficulty in learning new skills • Sunk costs • Lack of skills		**0**
Political	**Allocating power and resources** • Threat to the old guard from the new guard • Relationships • Power and authority imbalance or self-preservation	• Doesn't want to be watched so closely • Thinks the schedule may become too rigid	**60**
Cultural	**Articulating the glue or cultural norms** • Selective perception • Locked into old "mindset" • Afraid of letting go	• Doesn't want performance data tied to merit increases	**40**

Figure 4.13   TPC analysis for driver.

- Milestone review
- Project launch meeting
- Town hall for drivers
- Town hall for store receiving personnel
- Town hall for warehouse receiving/shipping personnel
- Town hall for vendor shipping personnel

This information was then used to develop a project communication plan. The plan consisted of three matrices. First was the RASIC, which documents the

Warehouse Rec. and Ship. Personnel			
Source of resistance	*Define causes of resistance*	*Examples from our project*	*Rating*
Technical	**Aligning and structuring organization** • Habit and inertia • Difficulty in learning new skills • Sunk costs • Lack of skiffs		0
Political	**Allocating power and resources** • Threat to the old guard from the new guard • Relationships • Power and authority imbalance or self-preservation	• Not happy to have transportation pushing warehouse personnel	20
Cultural	**Articulating the glue or cultural norms** • Selective perception • Locked into old "mindset" • Afraid of letting go	• Forced to work faster loading or unloading, may be unsafe and reduced quality • Reduced number of personnel per load or unload event	80

Figure 4.14   TPC analysis for warehouse receiving and shipping personnel.

responsibilities of the team members relative to the communication strategies, as shown in Figure 4.21. Here again the team noted responsibilities for future team members (added later, as shown in Figure 4.27). The next two matrices document which stakeholder is invited to an event (Figure 4.22) and which stakeholder received communications relative to the deliverables (Figure 4.23). By using these three documents, the team ensures that they keep all of the stakeholders up to date with the information

Vendor Shipping Personnel		Example from our project	Rating
Source of resistance	*Define causes of resistance*		
Technical	**Aligning and structuring organization** • Habit and inertia • Difficulty in learning new skills • Sunk costs • Lack of skills		
Political	**Allocating power and resources** • Threat to the old guard from the new guard • Relationships • Power and authority imbalance or self-preservation		
Cultural	**Articulating the glue or cultural norms** • Selective perception • Locked into old "mindset" • Afraid of letting go	• Worried that trailers will be taken at unpredictable or inconsistent times	**100**

Figure 4.15   TPC analysis for vendor shipping personnel.

relevant to them while offering them a chance to participate in the breakthrough process.

Perform Initial VOC and Identify CTS

Anita called the team together for a meeting to determine how to gather the initial voice of the customer (VOC). Robert suggested the team gather information from the process sponsor and core team discussion. Jim

Store Receiving Personnel			
Source of resistance	*Define causes of resistance*	*Examples from our project*	*Rating*
Technical	**Aligning and structuring organization** • Habit and inertia • Difficulty In learning new skills • Sunk costs • Lack of skills		
Political	**Allocating power and resources** • Threat to the old guard from the new guard • Relationships • Power and authority imbalance or self-preservation		
Cultural	**Articulating the glue or cultural norms** • Selective perception • Locked into old "mindset" • Afraid of letting go	Afraid new standards will be set for unloading trailers which are too difficult and dangerous	**100**

Figure 4.16   TPC analysis for store receiving personnel.

stated that this information could be used to develop the initial project scope. The team agreed that the initial VOC could also be used to drive the initial critical-to-satisfaction characteristics (CTS). So, the team began to brainstorm the needs of the stakeholders/customers and compiled a list that became the initial VOC, as shown in Figure 4.24.

Once the team gathered the initial VOC, Anita scheduled a brief meeting to determine the initial CTS characteristics, as shown in Figure 4.25. The team used the

Transportation Office

Stakeholders	Strongly Against	Moderate Against	Neutral	Moderate Support	Strongly Support	Comm. Strategy	Strategy Mgr.
General Manager					X...O	• Project Launch • Keep Informed • Advocate within Office	Team Member 1
Dispatch Manager		X			→O	• Project Launch • Invite at All Levels	Project Champ.
Driver Coordinator			X		→O	• Project Launch • Keep Informed • Invite to Reviews	Team Member 1
Driver			X		→O	• Inform of Project Launch • Keep Informed • Town Hall	Team Member 1

X = Current   O = Future

Figure 4.17 Customer/stakeholders matrix for transportation office.

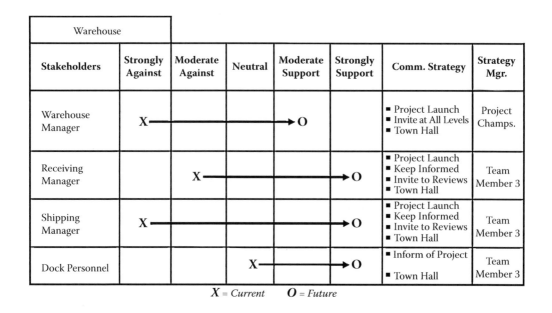

Figure 4.18   Customer/stakeholders matrix for warehouse.

Figure 4.19   Customer/stakeholders matrix for vendor.

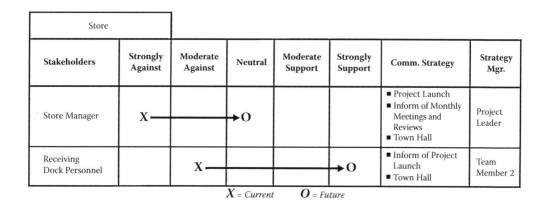

Figure 4.20   **Customer/stakeholders matrix for store.**

needs from the initial VOC and regrouped them into families that characterize one CTS factor. The factors were then summarized in the form of the CTS summary, as shown in Figure 4.26.

Select the Team and Launch the Project

Up to now, only the core team had been meeting and generating deliverables. The main foundation of the project was complete, but there would soon be a need for additional resources to help keep the project's momentum at the pace necessary to complete it in a reasonable time frame. A call was made for one volunteer from each transportation building within the Midwest region who was a stakeholder. Once volunteers stepped up, Anita put together an updated organization chart with the following additions (also shown in Figure 4.27):

Responsible (R) Approval (A) Support (S) Inform (I) Consult (C)	**Project Leader** *Anita Smith*	**Process Owner** *Robert Quincy*	**Project Champion** *Joe Thompson*	**CI Mentor/MBB** *Jim Pulls*	**Finance** *Joe Thompson*	**Team Member 1**	**Team Member 2**	**Team Member 3**	**Team Member 4**	**Team Member 5**	**Team Member 6**
Weekly Meeting	R	S	A	C	S	S	S	S	S	S	S
Send out the Agenda & Minutes	A					R					
Monthly Meeting	R	S	A	C	S	S	S	S	S	S	S
Send out the Agenda & Minutes	A					R					
Milestone Review	R	S	A	C	S	S	S	S	S	S	S
Send out a Copy of the Report	A					R					
Project Launch Meeting	S	S	R	A	S	S	S	S	S	S	S
Send out a Copy of the Report	A					R					
Town Hall (Web Mtg) 1—Driver	S	I	A/I	I	I	R	I	I	I	I	I
Town Hall (Web Mtg) 2—Store	S	I	A/I	I	I	I	R	I	I	I	I
Town Hall (Web Mtg) 3—Warehouse	S	I	A/I	I	I	I	I	R	I	I	I
Town Hall (Web Mtg) 4—Vendor	S	I	A/I	I	I	I	I	I	R	I	I
Final Report	R	S	A	C	S	S	S	S	S	S	S
Send out a Copy of the Report	A					R					

Figure 4.21   Communication plan—RASIC.

Midwest Logistics, Lean Six Sigma Team Additions

Team Member 1: Paul Jones, driver coordinator Midwest Transpo 1

Team Member 2: Dave Leader, dispatch manager Midwest Transpo 2

Team Member 3: Simone Fillbert, general manager Midwest Transpo 3

Team Member 4: Cindy Patch, dispatch manager Midwest Transpo 4

Team Member 5: Chris Roberts, driver coordinator
Midwest Transpo 5
Team Member 6: Mike O'Conner, dispatch manager
Midwest Transpo 6

At the first meeting with the full team, Anita made the first item of business to establish team member ground rules, as shown in Figure 4.28. This helped the team meetings run more smoothly and established expectations for participation and behavior.

Create Responsibility Matrix (RASIC)

The next item for discussion was the creation of the responsibility matrix for the full team. Anita directed the team to the activities and deliverables for the Define phase of the project. Here, the team began to assign responsibilities based on the roles each played on the team. The RASIC format was used to easily identify the roles. The new members noted that they could not be responsible for deliverables before their addition. To help with the process, Jim Pulls presented the team with the responsibility matrix, as shown in Figure 4.29.

Create Project Plan

The next task for the team was to set a project timeline and develop a project plan. For the project timeline, the team laid out the major phases of Lean Six Sigma (Define, Measure, Analyze, Improve, and Control) into a timeline, as shown in Figures 4.30 and 4.31. The timeline included

Level of Participation Invited (X)	Transportation General Mgrs.	Transportation Dispatch Mgrs.	Transportation Driver Coord.	Drivers	Warehouse General Mgrs.	Warehouse Rec. Mgrs.	Warehouse Shipping Mgrs.	Warehouse Dock Personnel	Vendor Operations Mgr.	Vendor Shipping Mgr.	Vendor Dock Personnel	Store General Mgrs.	Store Rec. Personnel
Weekly Meeting		X											
Monthly Meeting		X			X								
Milestone Review	X	X	X		X								
Project Launch Meeting	X	X	X		X	X	X		X	X		X	
Town Hall (Web Mtg) 1 - Driver				X									
Town Hall (Web Mtg) 2 - Store												X	X
Town Hall (Web Mtg) 3 - Warehouse					X	X	X	X					
Town Hall (Web Mtg) 4 - Vendor									X				
Final Report Presentation													

Figure 4.22 Communication plan matrix—events.

Method of Communication Hardcopy (H) Email (E)	Transportation General Mgrs.	Transportation Dispatch Mgrs.	Transportation Driver Coord.	Drivers	Warehouse General Mgrs.	Warehouse Rec Mgrs.	Warehouse Shipping Mgrs.	Warehouse Dock Personnel	Vendor Operations Mgr.	Vendor Shipping Mgr.	Vendor Dock Personnel	Store General Mgrs.	Store Rec. Personnel
Weekly Meeting Agenda & Minutes	E	E											
Monthly Meeting Agenda & Minutes	E	E	E	E	E	E	E					E	
Milestone Report	H	E	E	E	H	E	E		E			E	
Project Launch Report	H	E	E	E	H	E	E	E	E	E		E	E
Final Report	H	E	E	E	H	E	E	E	E			E	E

Figure 4.23   Communication plan matrix—deliverables.

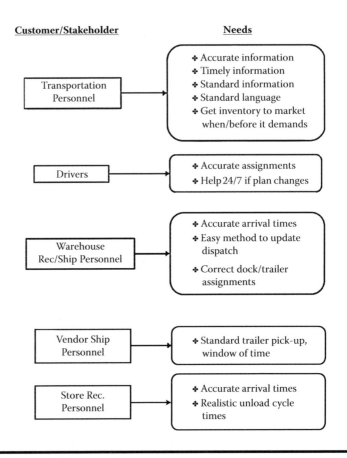

Figure 4.24   VOC needs diagram.

each phase activity, the time to accomplish those activities, and a date for submitting each phase report. A more detailed project plan was also developed by the team to highlight significant team events, their status, due dates, deliverables, and resources, as shown in Figure 4.32.

Before moving on to the Measure phase, Anita met with the team to review their accomplishments during the Define phase. She also announced the major tools the team would use in the Measure phase, including process maps, data collection plan, survey construction, database orientation, and data extraction sessions, as shown in Figure 4.33.

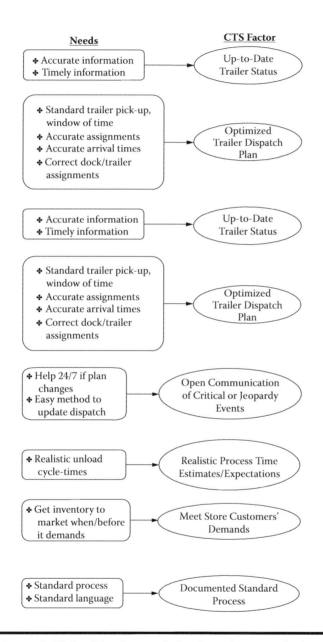

Figure 4.25 Initial critical to satisfaction characteristics.

- Up-to-Date Trailer Status
- Optimized Trailer Dispatch Plan
- Open Communication of Critical or Jeopardy Events
- Realistic Process Time Estimates/Expectations
- Meet Store Customers' Demands
- Documented Standard Process

Figure 4.26   Initial CTS characteristics summary.

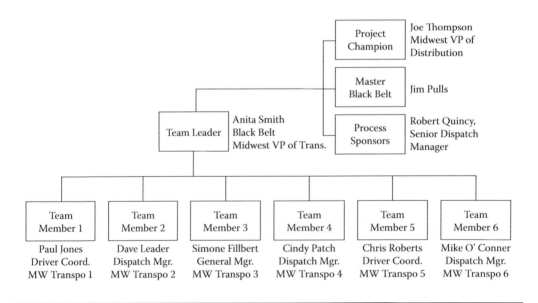

Figure 4.27   Project team organization.

- Everyone is responsible for the success of the project.
- Be on time and prepared.
- Be a team player.
- Respect each other's ideas.
- Question and participate.
- Respect differences.
- Keep an open mind and appreciate other points of view.
- Be willing to make mistakes or have a different opinion.
- Share your knowledge, experience, and time.
- Stay focused on the task and the person speaking.
- Communicate openly and don't assume someone knows what you know.
- Don't interrupt.
- Keep up-to-date.
- Have Fun!

Figure 4.28   Team member ground rules.

Responsible (R) / Approval (A) / Support (S) / Inform (I) / Consult (C)	Team Leader *Anita Smith*	Process Owner *Robert Quincy*	Project Champion *Joe Thompson*	CIMentor/MBB *Jim Pulls*	Finance *Joe Thompson*	Team Member1 *Paul Jones*	Team Member2 *Dave Leader*	Team Member *Simone Fillbert*	Team Member4 *Cindy Patch*	Team Member5 *Chris Roberts*	Team Member6 *Mike O'Conner*
Develop Initial Documents											
Form Core Team	R	I	A	A	C						
Define Activities and Deliverables for Define Phase	R	I	A	A	I						
Responsibility Matrix	R	I	A	C	I						
Project Charter	R	S	A	C	S						
SIPOC	R	S	A	C	I						
Identify Stakeholders & Communication Plan											
Stakeholder Analysis Matrix	R	S	A	C	S						
TPC Analysis	R	S	A	C	S						
Customers/Stakeholders Matrix	R	S	A	C	S						
Communication Plan	R	S	A	c	S						

Perform Initial VOC and Identify CTS									
CTS Summary	R	S	A	C	S				
Select Team and Launch the Project									
Team Organization Chart	R	S	A	C	S				
Revise Responsibility Matrix	R	I	A	C	I	S	S	S	S
Items for Resolution (IFR) Form	R	S	A	C	S	I	I	I	I
Establish Ground Rules	R	S	A	C	S	S	S	S	S
Create Project Plan									
Macro Project Plan	R	S	A	C	S	S	S	S	S

Figure 4.29   Responsibility matrix (RASIC).

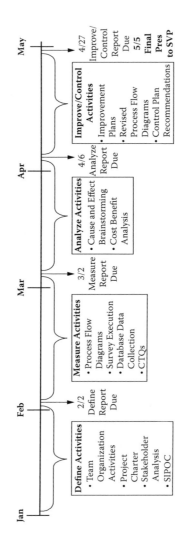

Figure 4.30   Macro project timeline.

Event	Dates
Form Core Team	Jan 4
Project Launch Meeting	Jan 23
Define Review	Feb 2–3
Town Hall—Drivers	Feb 5
Town Hall—Store	Feb 6
Town Hall—Warehouse	Feb 7
Town Hall—Vendor	Feb 8
Measure Presentation	Mar 2–3
Data Analysis Complete	Mar 30
Analyze Presentation	Apr 6–7
Cause and Effect Analysis Complete	Apr 23
Improve/Control Presentation	Apr 27–28
Final Report/Presentation	May 5–6

Figure 4.31   Project plan events.

	Activity	Status	Due Date	Deliverables	Resources
	Define Phase				
1	Form Core Team	Complete	1/4	Organizational Chart	
2	Define Activities and Deliverables	Complete	1/6	Activities and Deliverables Matrix	
3	Define Responsibilities	Complete	1/6	Responsibility Matrix	
4	Prepare Project Charter	Complete	1/10	Project Charter	
5	Define High Level Process Flow and Participants	Complete	1/10	SIPOC	
6	Define Customer / Stakeholder	Complete	1/15	Stakeholder Analysis Matrix, TPC Analysis, Customer/ Stakeholder Analysis	
7	Define Communication Plan	Complete	1/16	Communications Plan	
8	Perform Initial VOC and Identify CTS	Complete	1/17	CTS Summary	
9	Select Additional Team Members	Complete	1/18	Update Organizational Chart	
10	Revise Responsibilities	Complete	1/19	Update Responsibility Matrix	
11	Develop Method to Control Change	Complete	1/19	Items for Resolution Form	
12	Prepare Project Plan	Complete	1/20	Project Plan	
13	Prepare Define Phase Report and Presentation	Complete	2/2	Define Phase Report	

Figure 4.32   Project plan—define.

■ Measure Phase
  – Process Maps
  – Data Collection Plan
  – Survey Construction
  – Database Orientation
  – Data Extraction Session

Figure 4.33 Measure phase steps.

Chapter 5

Measure Phase

Introduction

With the Define phase complete, the Lean Six Sigma team now had a clear understanding of what was to be done, how they were going to do it, and who was responsible for getting it done. The team had also developed a valuable understanding of the stakeholders and their level of resistance to the change. In addition, there was a communications plan to ensure that all members and stakeholders had opportunities to exchange ideas and allow for the voice of the customer to be heard. Now it was time to move on.

Within the Measure phase, the team must further define the processes that it is going to study, so that a plan can be built that covers what data exists within the process and what data they must collect. Concurrently, the team will collect the voice of the customer, which is impacted by the trailer utilization process. Through interviews, focus groups, and surveys, the VOC will appear. Then, once the data has been collected, the voice of the process (VOP) is defined, which sets the baseline for the process. To ensure that the data collected is not biased by the collection instrument or methods, they will need to validate the instruments and methods that were used. So, let's get back to the case.

As preparation for the first meeting of the Measure phase, Anita sent the team members a list of questions that she used as a basis for the meeting's discussion.

■ What are the key metrics for the business process?
■ Are the metrics valid and reliable?
■ Do we have adequate data on this process?
■ How will we measure progress?
■ How will we measure ultimate success?

The team's next effort was to document the current process. This included the process itself and all inputs and outputs as they were at the time of recording. Validation of the measurement process was also necessary. Jim Pulls had helped Anita put together a list of deliverables relative to the activities that were planned for this phase. Figure 5.1 shows each item as planned. One of the team members, Simone Fillbert, asked why they were doing a survey. Wouldn't the data from the Logistics department be enough? Anita and Joe both agreed that the data only shows some of the areas for improvement. They explained that knowing the voice of the customer was important for finding variation, but it can also lead to discoveries that the database data does not document.

Define the Current Process

Cindy Patch, Chris Roberts, and Anita were tasked with defining the current process. Before they started to

Measure Activities	Deliverables
1 Define the current process	1) Process Map
	2) Data Collection Plan, Metrics, and Operational Definitions
	3) Baseline
2 Define the detailed VOC	4) Interviews and Focus Groups
	5) Affinity Diagrams
	6) Translate Needs to CTQ
	7) Survey and Results
	8) Customer Needs Map (CNM)
	9) Quality Functional Deployment (QFD) Diagram
3 Define the voice of process and current performance	10) CTS-Factor-Operational Definition-Metric-Target Mapping
	11) Benchmarking
	12) Check Sheets
	13) Pareto Charts, Time Series, Histograms, Box Plots, Capability and Statistics
4 Validate measurement system	14) Measurement System Analysis and Gauge R&R
5 Define COPQ and Cost/Benefit	15) Cost of Poor Quality

Figure 5.1   Measure phase activities and deliverables.

define the current process, Jim Pulls decided that the group might need some help understanding what they were to define. With the help of Robert Quincy, the team members put together a service flowdown diagram and a process flowdown diagram (Figures 5.2 and 5.3). These diagrams provided some guidance of who they were to interview and what functions they were to focus on. This is also commonly called a *product flowdown*. These items help define the Y's (outputs) for the service or product

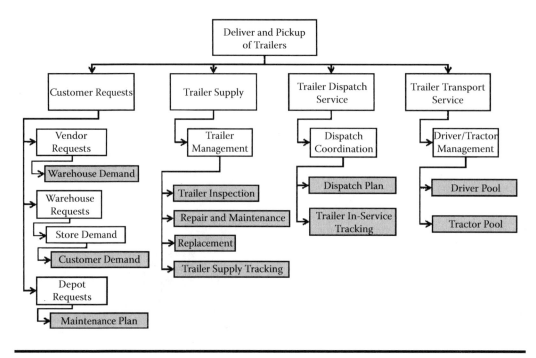

Figure 5.2   Service flowdown diagram.

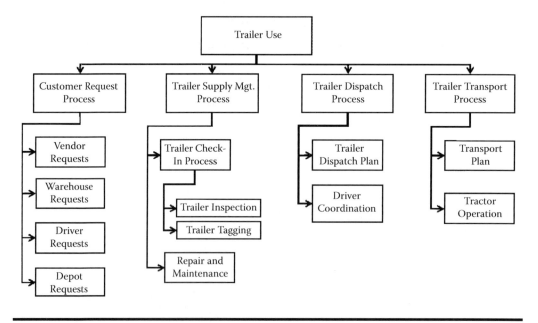

Figure 5.3   Process flowdown diagram.

via specifications or critical-to-X (CTX) characteristics. A CTX is a general term used to optimize a key measurable characteristic that is "critical to" performance or customer expectation. The reason to look at this flowdown is to examine the element critical-to-quality (CTQ) characteristics. Similarly, CTQs are critical quality parameters within a process to ensure that the customer requirements are met. The CTQ and CTS characteristics should be logically related. If not, they require further examination to ensure customer needs are truly met.

So began their investigation, which involved interviews, standard-operating-procedure reviews, and general observations to be conducted by each team member. The group started with some basic facts on the region and then got into the details by listing the processes related to trailer utilization, as shown in Figure 5.4.

- Trailer Request
  - Vendor
  - Warehouse
  - Driver (see trailer use map)
  - Depot
- Trailer Check-In (Depot)
- Dispatch Plan Maintenance (Driver Coordinator)
- Trailer Transport (Driver)
  - Long Haul
  - Depot–Warehouse–Depot (D–W–D)

Figure 5.4 Processes related to trailer utilization.

The transportation office coordinates the movement of trailers within specified regions. Within each region, there are vendors, warehouses, stores, and depots. The depot serves as a central location to store, repair, and maintain trailers. The following is a list of the resources and facts that the team thought were important to the trailer utilization process:

- 12,544 trailers
- 6 transportation offices
- 6 warehouses
- 6 depots
- 1,500 stores receiving 24 × 7
- 148 vendors, some with limited dock hours and days
- 6,000 drivers with a maximum workday of 14 hours
- 240 driver coordinators work four 12-hr shifts to cover 24 × 7

The flow of trailers is represented in Figure 5.5. Note that the route between the depot and the warehouse is designated as the depot–warehouse–depot (D–W–D) route, and only designated drivers handle this route. All of the other trailer routes are considered long-haul routes, while the D–W–D route is sometimes referred to as the short-haul route.

Figure 5.6 shows a typical long-haul trailer process. Here the request is received by the driver coordinator, who then dispatches a driver to a full-trailer pickup. The trailer is transported to a store where it is unloaded. The "live unload" designates that the driver stays with the trailer instead of dropping it off. Once the trailer is unloaded, the driver transports the empty back to the depot.

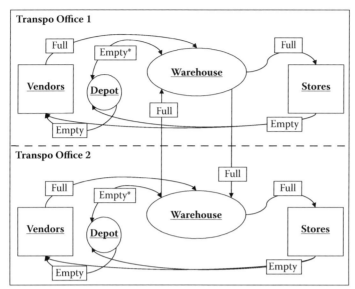

*Note: This route is designated as "Depot-Warehouse-Depot" (D-W-D)

Figure 5.5   Flow of trailers.

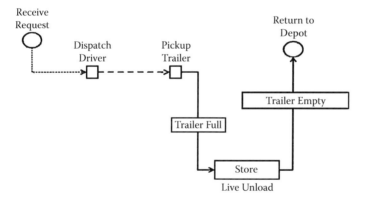

Figure 5.6   Typical long-haul trailer process.

The team found that the trailer dispatch process relied on the documentation of the status of drivers and the status of the trailer requests, so that it could ensure that trailers were picked up or dropped off as requested. Figure 5.7 is an example of the Driver's Board database. A driver was either on the road as full, empty, or with no trailer. If

	Last Name	Number	Status
D1	Raber	555-231-9089	Empty
D2	Haas	555-231-5643	Full
D3	Lewellen	555-231-0007	Full
D4	Pauls	555-354-1786	Empty
D5	Phillipie	555-231-0908	Ready
D6	Vasco	555-432-0978	No Trailer
D7	Rance	555-354-2376	Off Duty
D8	Smitty	555-231-0793	D–W–D
D9	O'Conner	555-432-9090	Full

Figure 5.7   Driver's board database.

a driver was waiting on an assignment, the driver's status was changed to "Ready." If the driver was the designated D–W–D, it was noted, as well as if the driver was off duty.

To track the requests for trailers, the driver coordinators log each request and all of the actions necessary to get the trailer to its request by means of the Trailer Log database. This is a computer-based system that stores the data on trailer requests. The coordinator opens a new request number for each new request and completes the fields as the driver is dispatched through and up to the point where the trailer is docked. The team sees this data as very powerful. Figure 5.8 shows an example of the data stored by request. The team can follow a driver and the trailer as it moves through the process. In request 1001, trailer 12004 is full and docked at a store. Once there, it is unloaded and returned via request 1006 to the Depot (shown in the row labeled Driver in Figure 5.8 by following D1).

Request	1001	1002	1003	1004	1005	1006	1007	1008	1009	1010	1011	1012	1013
Time	6/2/2008 13:42	6/2/2008 13:45	6/2/2008 14:00	6/2/2008 14:09	6/2/2008 14:09	6/2/2008 18:38	6/2/2008 18:40	6/2/2008 18:45	6/2/2008 19:00	6/2/2008 18:38	6/2/2008 18:40	6/2/2008 18:45	6/2/2008 19:00
Request By	Ware	Ware	Vendor	Vendor	Driver	Driver	Driver	Ware	Depot	Driver	Driver	Ware	Depot
Dispatch	13:59												
Driver	D1	D2	D3	D4	D6	D1	D3	D8	D8	D1	D3	D8	D8
Trailer	12004	987	7789	6745	0	12004	13288	13456	789	12004	13288	13456	789
Pickup Dock	23	34	L1	13	0	3	10	L2	21	5	10	L2	21
Dest. Dock	3	1	S12	5	DR	CHKIN	35	23	Shop	CHKIN	35	23	Shop
Mode A	Full	Full	Empty	Empty	No Trailer	Empty	Full	Empty	Empty	Empty	Full	Empty	Empty
Mode B	Live	Drop	Drop	Drop	None	Drop	Drop	Drop	Drop	Drop	Drop	Drop	Drop
Mode C	Origin	Origin	Origin	Connect	Return	Return	Return	D-W-D	D-W-D	Return	Return	D-W-D	D-W-D
Mode D	Long	Long	Long	Long	Long	Long	Long	D-W-D	D-W-D	Long	Long	D-W-D	D-W-D
From	W	W	D	S	S	S	V	D	W	S	V	D	W
To	S	S	V	V	D	D	W	W	D	D	W	W	D
ETL	6/2/2008 14:00												
Depart	6/2/2008 14:05												
ETA	6/2/2008 19:00	6/3/2008 7:00	6/2/2008 18:00	6/3/2008 8:00	6/3/2008 7:00	6/3/2008 8:00	6/3/2008 7:00	6/2/2008 19:30		6/3/2008 8:00	6/3/2008 7:00	6/2/2008 19:30	
Call In	6/2/2008 18:10												
Dest. Docked	6/2/2008 18:38		6/2/2008 18:40					6/2/2008 19:10				6/2/2008 19:10	
Notes			Pickup 13288	Pickup 01998	Drop Only				P/M				P/M

(D = Depot, S = Store, V = Vendor, W = Warehouse) (Mode A = Trailer Condition, Mode B = Trailer State at Dest., Mode C = Leg of trip, Mode D = Type of Transit)

Figure 5.8   Example of the data stored by request.

Process Mapping

The team now had some basic facts and access to and understanding of the Driver's Board and the Trailer Plan log. Instead of trying to use these items to piece together the process, they decided to interview some relevant stakeholders and reference any standard operating procedures that were being used to help them build the process maps. The interviews and research culminated in a written process, which then was converted to process maps. Their work appears in the following sections. The team listed the steps for each process and then drew process flow diagrams.

Trailer Request by Warehouse (Figure 5.9)

1. Daily shipping request is sent to warehouse by store.
2. Warehouse begins to assemble the order at a specific dock.
3. Warehouse requests an empty trailer, if one is not already at the dock.
4. If the trailer is at the dock, the shipping dock personnel begin loading the trailer.
5. Once it is full, a request is placed with the transportation office for pickup and delivery.

Trailer Request by Vendor (Figure 5.10)

1. Weekly shipping request is sent to vendor by warehouse.
2. Vendor begins to assemble the order at a specific dock.
3. Vendor requests an empty trailer, if one is not already at the dock.

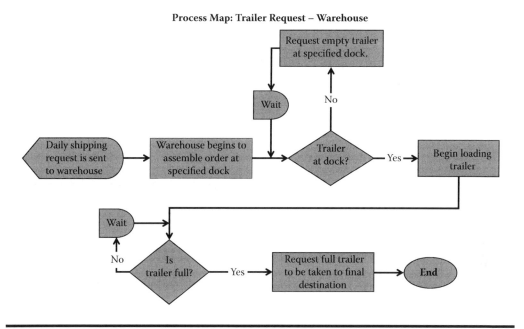

Figure 5.9 **Trailer request by warehouse.**

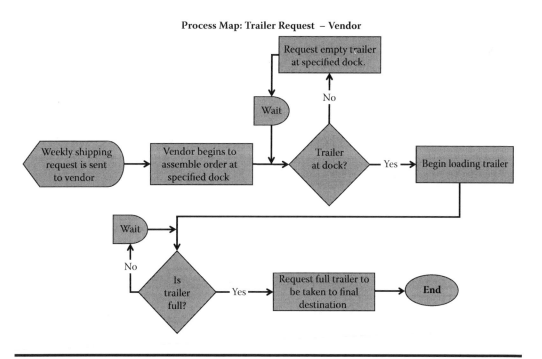

Figure 5.10 **Trailer request by vendor.**

4. If the trailer is at the dock, the shipping dock personnel begin loading the trailer.

5. Once it is full, a request is placed with the transportation office for pickup and delivery.

Trailer Request by Depot (Figure 5.11)

1. Depot personnel print out the daily maintenance plan report.

2. From the report, a list of trailers scheduled for preventive maintenance (P/M) or those to be decommissioned are identified.

3. Depot requests the trailer if it is not in the depot's yard.

4. If the trailer is scheduled for P/M, it is moved to the garage for service.

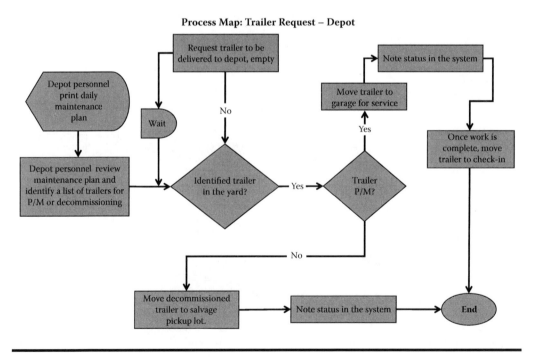

Figure 5.11   Trailer request by depot.

   a. If P/M is scheduled, then once in the garage, the trailer's status is logged as "shop," and service begins. Once the work is complete, the trailer is moved to trailer check-in.

   b. If no P/M is scheduled, then the trailer must be from the other category on the list, decommissioning. The trailer is moved to the salvage pickup lot, and the status is changed in the system to "decom."

Trailer Check-In (Figure 5.12)

1. Trailer dropped off at depot by driver.
2. Trailer checked in by depot staff.
3. Trailer cleaned and inspected.

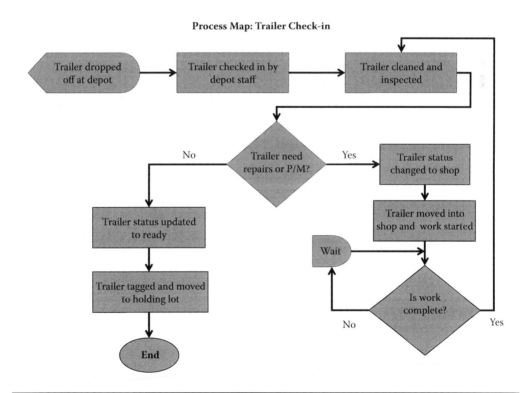

Figure 5.12   Trailer check-in.

4. If the trailer needs repairs or P/M, the trailer status is changed to "Shop" and moved into the shop area.

   a. If repairs or P/M are scheduled, the work is completed in the shop area. Once completed, the trailer is again cleaned and inspected.

   b. If no repairs or P/M are scheduled, the trailer status is updated to "Ready," and the trailer is moved to the holding lot.

Dispatch Plan Maintenance (Figure 5.13)

1. Driver coordinator receives a trailer request.

2. Coordinator opens a request and inputs all given information.

3. If the request is for an empty trailer delivery, the trailer could be delivered to a warehouse, vendor, or depot.

   a. If the empty trailer delivery is to a warehouse, the driver coordinator dispatches the driver who is on Depot–Warehouse–Depot (D–W–D) duty. The coordinator communicates the pickup and destination docks and requests the estimated time of arrival (ETA), trailer number, and departure time from the D–W–D driver. Once the D–W–D driver replies with the ETA, the coordinator updates the Trailer Plan log. Soon after, the driver calls in with the trailer number, and the coordinator follows by updating the log. The driver then calls in the departure time to the coordinator, who again updates the log. Due to the short distance, the call-in time will be the same as the departure time.

Process Map: Dispatch Plan Maintenance

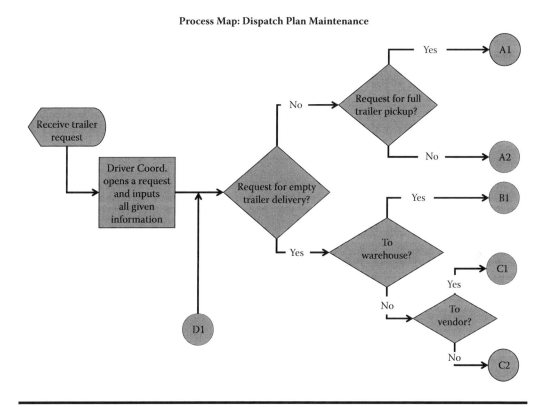

Figure 5.13 Dispatch plan maintenance.

The D–W–D driver will communicate the time the trailer was docked at its destination, so the coordinator can update the log and complete the request.

b. If empty trailer delivery is to a vendor, the driver coordinator follows the Standard Long-Haul Dispatch procedure.

Standard Long-Haul Dispatch Procedure

i. If a request is made by a driver, then skip to step ii. If the request is made by any-one other than a driver, then the driver coordinator checks the Driver Board for

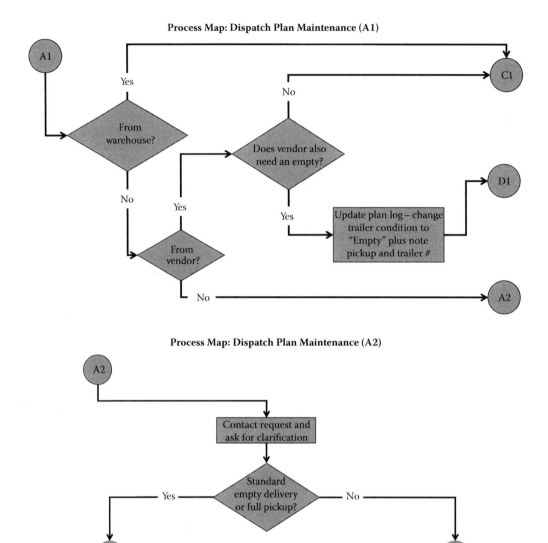

Figure 5.13   (continued).

driver availability. If there are drivers ready, the coordinator dispatches a driver. If no drivers are ready, they wait for a driver to call in.

ii. Once a driver is dispatched or it is verified that the requester is a driver, then the

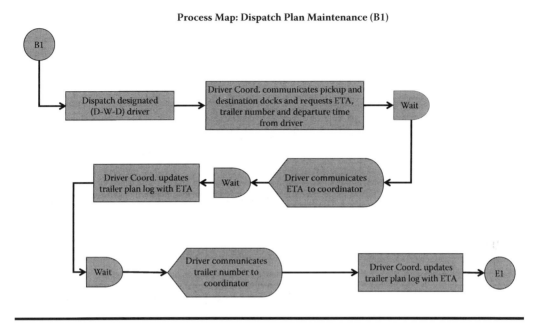

Process Map: Dispatch Plan Maintenance (B1)

Figure 5.13 (continued).

coordinator communicates the travel plan, pickup and destination docks, estimated time of leave (ETL), and the estimated time of arrival while requesting the trailer number and departure time from the driver. Once the trailer departs, the driver calls in the trailer number and departure time for the coordinator to log. When the driver reaches the destination's staging zone, the driver calls in to update the trailer's location and confirms the destination dock number. The coordinator confirms the dock number and logs the driver's call-in time. Once the trailer is docked, the driver reports the trailer's dock time, so that the coordinator can update the log and close out the request.

Process Map: Dispatch Plan Maintenance (C1)

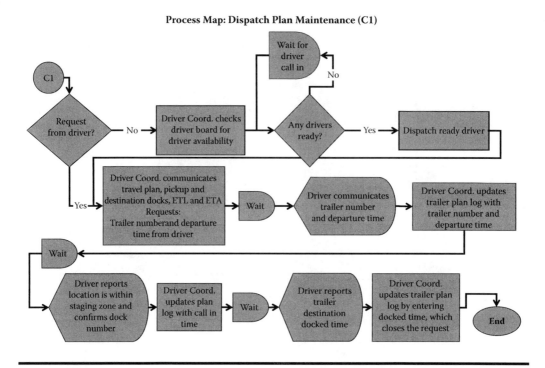

Figure 5.13 (continued).

c. If the empty trailer delivery is to a depot and the route is a long-haul route, the driver coordinator follows the Standard Long-Haul Dispatch procedure (see section b). If it is not a long-haul route, then the driver coordinator dispatches the driver who is on Depot–Warehouse–Depot (D–W–D) duty. The coordinator communicates the trailer number and the pickup and destination docks and then requests the estimated time of leave (ETL) and the departure time from the D–W–D driver. Once the D–W–D driver replies with the ETL, the coordinator updates the Trailer Plan log. The driver then calls in the departure time to the coordinator, who then updates the log. Due to the short

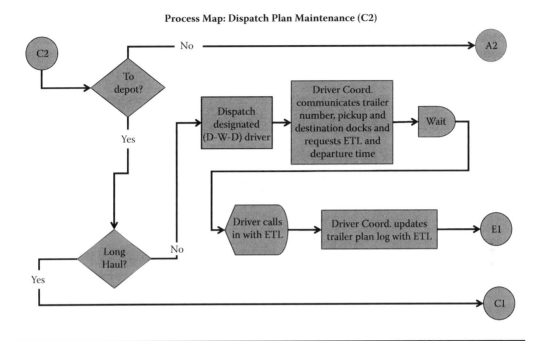

Process Map: Dispatch Plan Maintenance (C2)

Figure 5.13   (continued).

distance, the call-in time will be the same as the departure time. The D–W–D driver will communicate the time the trailer was docked at its destination, so the coordinator can update the log and complete the request.

d. If the empty trailer delivery is not to a warehouse, vendor, or depot, the driver coordinator must contact the requester to ask for clarification. If the request is indeed for a standard empty delivery or a full pickup (maybe the request was not clear or complete), then go back to step 3 of the Dispatch Plan Maintenance procedure. If it is not a standard empty delivery or a full pickup, then this would be classified as a special request. Is the special request within Logistics' means?

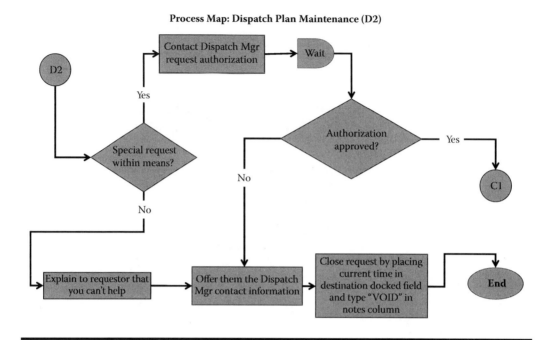

Figure 5.13   (continued).

If so, contact the dispatch manager for authorization. If authorization has been approved, the Standard Long-Haul Dispatch procedure can be used. If there is no authorization, offer the requester the dispatch manager's contact information and then close out the request by placing the current time in the destination docked field and typing "VOID" in the notes field. If the special request is not within Logistics' means, then contact the requester and explain. Then offer the requester the dispatch manager's contact information and close out the request by placing the current time in the destination docked field and typing "VOID" in the notes field.

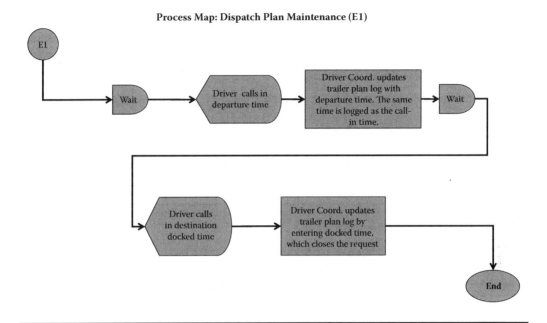

Process Map: Dispatch Plan Maintenance (E1)

Figure 5.13 (continued).

4. If the request is for a full trailer pickup (and transport), the trailer could be picked up from a warehouse or a vendor.

   a. If a full trailer pickup request is from a warehouse, the driver coordinator uses the Standard Long-Haul Dispatch procedure.

   b. If a full trailer pickup request is from a vendor, the driver coordinator must confirm if the vendor needs an empty. If an empty trailer is required, then change the trailer request to empty delivery, and type "pickup needed" and the trailer number in the notes field. Then go back to step 3 in the Dispatch Plan Maintenance procedure with a request for an empty trailer delivery. If an empty trailer is not required, then follow the Standard Long-Haul Dispatch procedure.

    c. If a full-trailer pickup request is not from a warehouse or a vendor, the driver coordinator must contact the requester to ask for clarification. If the request is indeed for a standard empty delivery or a full pickup (maybe the request was not clear or complete), then go back to step 3 of the Dispatch Plan Maintenance procedure. If it is not a standard empty delivery or a full pickup, then this would be classified as a special request. Is the special request within Logistics' means? If so, contact the dispatch manager for authorization. If authorization has been approved, the Standard Long-Haul Dispatch procedure can be used. If there is no authorization, offer the requester the dispatch manager's contact information and then close out the request by placing the current time in the destination docked field and typing "VOID" in the notes field. If the special request is not within Logistics' means, then contact the requester and explain. Then offer the requester the dispatch manager's contact information and close out the request by placing the current time in the destination docked field and typing "VOID" in the notes field.

5. If the request is not for an empty trailer delivery or a full trailer pickup (and transport), then the driver coordinator must contact the requester to ask for clarification. If the request is indeed for a standard empty delivery or a full pickup (maybe the request was not clear or complete), then go back to step 3 of the Dispatch Plan Maintenance

procedure. If it is not a standard empty delivery or a full pickup, then this would be classified as a special request. Is the special request within Logistics' means? If so, contact the dispatch manager for authorization. If authorization has been approved, the Standard Long-Haul Dispatch procedure can be used. If there is no authorization, offer the requester the dispatch manager's contact information and then close out the request by placing the current time in the destination docked field and typing "VOID" in the notes field. If the special request is not within Logistics' means, then contact the requester and explain. Then offer the requester the dispatch manager's contact information and close out the request by placing the current time in the destination docked field and typing "VOID" in the notes field.

Trailer Long-Haul Process (Figure 5.14)
1. Driver is ready for dispatch.
2. Driver coordinator communicates travel plan, pickup and destination docks, estimated time to leave, and estimated time to arrive, and requests trailer number and departure time from the driver.
3. If the trailer is not ready, the driver contacts the driver coordinator and provides an update on the delay. Once the trailer is ready, then the driver secures the load and picks up the shipping documents.
4. The driver confirms the shipping documents are complete and then communicates the trailer number and departure time to the driver coordinator.

Process Map: Trailer Long Haul

Figure 5.14   Trailer long-haul process.

5. The driver then transports the trailer to the destination's staging zone.

6. Once within the staging zone, the driver contacts the destination receiving personnel to confirm the dock and arrival time if it is a full trailer. If the trailer is empty, the driver contacts the destination shipping personnel to confirm the shipping dock and arrival time.

7. Once contact has been established with the destination dock, the driver contacts the driver coordinator to report the trailer location (within the staging zone) and then makes a trailer request for a return or connecting trip.

8. The driver coordinator then communicates the return or connecting trip's travel plans, pickup

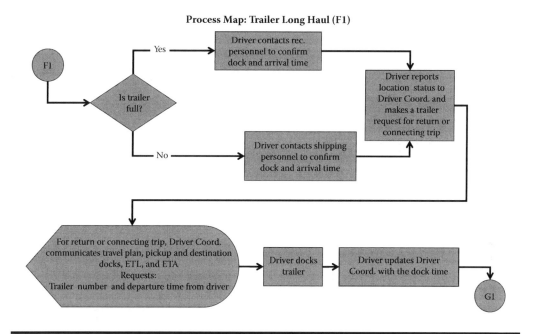

Figure 5.14 (continued).

and destination docks, ETL, and ETA, and requests that the driver reply with the trailer number and the departure time. (Typically this all happens before the origin trailer has docked.)

9. Then the driver docks the trailer and updates the driver coordinator with the dock time.

10. The driver hands off the shipping documents to the dock personnel.

11. The unload process could be a live unload or a drop 'n' hook.

    a. If this is a live unload, the driver waits for the unload process to complete.

    b. If it is a drop 'n' hook, the driver leaves the full trailer at the destination dock and picks up an empty trailer at the same destination.

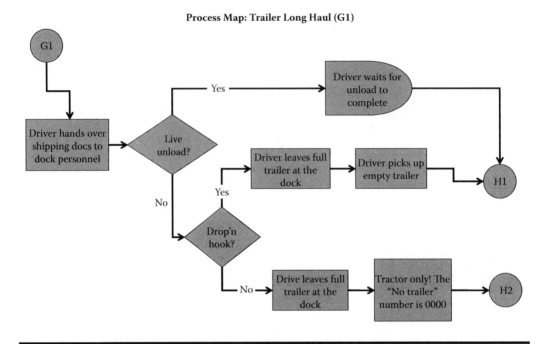

Process Map: Trailer Long Haul (G1)

Figure 5.14   (continued).

c. If it is not a live unload or a drop 'n' hook, then the driver leaves the full trailer at the dock. The trailer number for the return trip is "0000." The driver then communicates the trailer number and departure time to the driver coordinator. The driver then transports the tractor back to the depot staging zone. The driver then updates the coordinator with location and then later with the arrival (or dock time). This ends the long-haul process.

12. The driver secures the load for the return or connecting trip.

13. The driver then picks up any shipping documents and confirms they are complete.

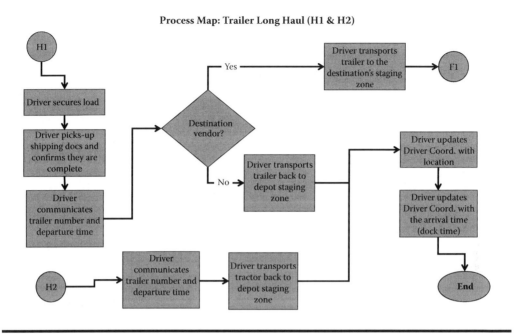

Figure 5.14 (continued).

14. The driver then communicates to the coordinator the trailer number and the departure time.
15. The next route could be to a vendor.
    a. If the route is to a vendor, the driver transports the trailer to the vendor's staging zone. The driver then goes back to step 6 of the Trailer Long-Haul process.
    b. If the destination is not to a vendor, then the default is to return to the depot. The driver transports the trailer back to the depot's staging zone. The driver then updates the coordinator with the location and then later with the arrival (or dock time). This ends the Trailer Long-Haul process.

Trailer Depot–Warehouse–Depot (D–W–D) Process
(Figure 5.15)

1. The driver is ready for dispatch or is in the process of completing a request.

2. The driver coordinator dispatches the D–W–D driver to deliver an empty trailer to the warehouse or to the depot.

    a. If delivery of the empty trailer is to the warehouse, the driver coordinator communicates the pickup and destination docks and requests the trailer number, ETA, and departure time from the driver. The driver replies with an ETA, and once at the depot yard, the driver can communicate the trailer number. The driver secures the trailer and then communicates the departure time to the coordinator. The trailer is transported to the destination dock, and then the driver communicates the destination time once the trailer is docked. This ends the Trailer D–W–D process.

    b. If the delivery of the empty trailer is not to the warehouse, then assume it is to the depot. The driver coordinator communicates the trailer number and pickup and destination docks and requests the driver to call in with the ETL and departure time. The driver calls back with the ETL and then proceeds to the pickup dock. The driver secures the trailer and then calls in the departure time. The driver transports the trailer to the depot check-in location. Once at the depot, the driver calls in the destination dock time. This ends the Trailer D–W–D process.

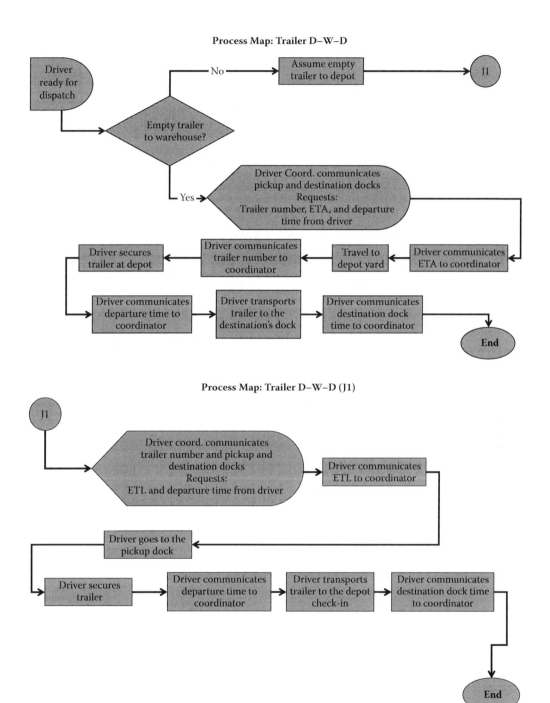

Figure 5.15 **Trailer depot–warehouse–depot (D-W-D) process.**

Data Collection Plan, Metrics, and Operational Definitions

After the process maps had been completed, the team came together to begin forming the data collection plan. The team had decided to leave out any data relative to the D–W–D process, because trailer utilization cannot be significantly improved during this process. D–W–D is only a process of moving empty trailers. They also decided that a separate project to improve the D–W–D process should be the focus of a different team.

Jim Pulls was notified of the scope change and congratulated them on their decision. Further, he advised the team to put together a System Model Map to help them define the metrics to be measured for trailer utilization. These metrics would then be transferred into the data collection plan. He provided a reference System Model Map of a typical supply chain process, as shown in Figure 5.16. The goal was to come up with metrics for the inputs and outputs specific to the trailer utilization process. The example Jim provided gave high-level categories to which they could match existing metrics or create new metrics. By doing this, they could easily see the inputs, or Xs, and outputs, or Ys, that will be needed for the Analyze phase.

Some of the metrics that the team came up with were currently used in the process, such as leave-on-schedule percentage (LOS%) and arrive-on-schedule percentage (AOS%). A few were new and needed to be measured, while some others were being logged in the Trailer Plan log database. The data collection plan was then used to

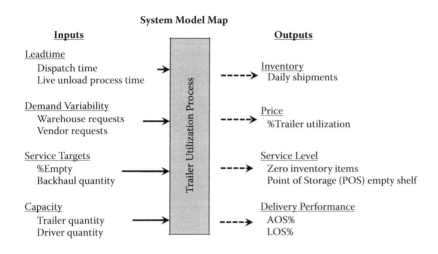

Figure 5.16   System Model map of a typical supply chain process.

help sort out what needed to be measured relative to the critical-to-satisfaction (CTS) characteristics, as shown in Figure 5.17. Because the data collection plan had limited room, each metric was then defined further in a separate document, as shown in Figure 5.18. Each metric was defined in greater detail, and the measurement type and data type were noted.

Beyond the metric definitions, the team put together operational definitions for each metric, as shown in Figure 5.19. It was important to define the metric, document the purpose for measuring the metric, and define the method to measure the metric. Anita made sure that everybody understood the importance of this step. If they did not define the method of measurement well, the metric would not be very repeatable, and this would add more variation to what they were originally trying to measure.

Critical to Satisfaction (CTS)	Metric	Data collection mechanism (survey, interview, focus group, etc.)	Analysis mechanism (statistics, statistical tests, etc.)	Sampling plan (sample size, sample frequency)	Sampling instructions (who, where, when, how)
Up-to-date trailer status	• Trailer Status • Trailer Status Error Rate	• Trailer Plan Log • Audit of Trailer Status Report	• Histograms • Pareto charts • Basic statistics • Hypothesis tests	• All trailers logged within the Trailer Plan Log • Audit random 5% for errors.	• Extracted from database within last 12 months. • Call site "given" to confirm trailer# & presence
Optimized trailer dispatch plan	• %Trailer Utilization • Daily Shipments • % Empty • AOS% & LOS% • Mean Dispatch • Mean Dev. from target: Dispatch. Arrival and Depart	• Trailer Plan Log	• Histograms • Pareto charts • Basic statistics • Hypothesis tests	• All trailers logged within the Trailer Plan Log	• Extracted from database within last 12 months
Open communication of critical or Jeopardy events	• % responded by question	• Survey	• Pareto analysis	• 5 Stakeholder groups	• Needs survey by email
Realistic Process time estimates—expectations	• Mean Dispatch Time • Live Unload Process Time	• Trailer Plan Log • Study	• Histograms • Pareto charts • Basic statistics • Hypothesis tests	• All requests logged within the Trailer Plan Log • 3 trucks by 10 stores by 3 times each store	• Extracted from database within last 12 months. • Team member to perform study at 10 stores within region
Meet store customers' demands	• Zero Inventory items per store • POS Empty Shelf per store	• Store Databases • Point of storage survey	• Histograms • Pareto charts • Basic statistics • Hypothesis tests	• All stores within region	• Extracted from database within last 12 months. • Download from POS, 2 weeks
Documented standard process	• Existing SOP% • Knowledge of Existing SOP%	• Audit • Survey	• Pareto charts • Basic statistics • Hypothesis tests	• All trailer utilization processes • 5 Stakeholder groups	• Team member to audit • Needs survey by email

Figure 5.17 Data collection plan.

CTS	Metric
Up-to-Date Trailer Status	**Trailer Status**—Data is the logged "real-time" location of a trailer. Qualitative measure and nominal data type. **Trailer Status Error Rate**—A calculated percentage of the incorrect trailer status tally by the total trailers audited. Quantitative, continuous measure, and ratio data.
Optimized Trailer Dispatch Plan	**% Trailer Utilization**—A percentage of total trailer hours used per day by total trailer hours available per day. Quantitative, continuous measure, and ratio data. **Daily Shipments**—Total shipments per day. Quantitative, discrete measure, and ratio data. **% Empty**—Calculated percentage of empty shipments by total shipments within one day. Quantitative, continuous measure, and ratio data. **Arrive On Schedule%**—A calculated percentage of shipments that arrive on time by total shipments per day. Quantitative, continuous measure, and ratio data. **Leave On Schedule%**—A calculated percentage of shipments that leave on time by total shipments per day. Quantitative, continuous measure, and ratio data. **Dispatch Mean**—A calculated average of dispatch time in minutes by day. Quantitative, continuous measure, and ratio data. **Dispatch Deviation Mean**—A calculated average of dispatch time deviations from a set target (30 minutes) in minutes. Negative is early and positive is late. Quantitative, continuous measure, and ratio data. **Arrival Deviation Mean**—A calculated average of arrival time deviations from ETA target in minutes. Negative is early and positive is late. Quantitative, continuous measure, and ratio data. **Departure Deviation Mean**—A calculated average of departure time deviations from ETL target in minutes. Negative is early and positive is late. Quantitative, continuous measure, and ratio data.

Figure 5.18 Definition of metrics.

CTS	Metric
Open communication of critical or jeopardy events	**% responded by question**—Percentage of the number of positive responses relative to survey question by total responses. Quantitative, continuous measure, and ratio data.
Realistic process time estimates/ expectations	**Live Unload process time**—Total time to unload a trailer at a store. Quantitative, continuous measure, and ratio data. **Dispatch Mean**—A calculated average of dispatch time in minutes by day. Quantitative, continuous measure, and ratio data.
Meet store customers' demands	**Zero-inventory items per store**—A daily total of merchandise that is at a zero quantity divided by the total number of stores. Quantitative, continuous measure, and ratio data. **POS Empty Shelf per store**—A daily total of survey results from customers who are reporting that they did not purchase an item due to an empty shelf per store. Quantitative, continuous measure, and ratio data.
Documented standard process	**Existing SOP%**—A percentage of formal SOPs in place by total SOPs possible. Quantitative, continuous measure, and ratio data. **% Knowledge of Existing SOP**—Percentage of the number of positive responses relative to survey question by total responses. Quantitative, continuous measure, and ratio data.

Figure 5.18 (continued).

Operational Definitions

Defining the Measure

<u>Trailer Status</u>—Data is the logged "real-time" location of a trailer. Qualitative measure and nominal data type.

Purpose

To document where trailers are at a snapshot in time. This data will be used for an audit to generate the Trailer Status Error metric.

Clear way to measure the process

Extracted from Trailer Plan Log at the time of the audit. The data is not recorded, but will be temporarily displayed on the PC screen during the audit.

Operational Definitions

Defining the Measure

<u>Trailer Status Error Rate</u>—A calculated percentage of the incorrect trailer status tally by the total trailers audited. Quantitative, continuous measure, and ratio data.

Purpose

Used to determine the accuracy of the current reporting method for Trailer Accounting.

Clear way to measure the process

Trailer status data is extracted from Trailer Plan Log in real-time during the audit. A random list of 5% of the trailers will be used to choose the trailers to audit. The Correct status and Incorrect status will be gathered by means of a check sheet.The audit will start and continue until completed (total time 52 hours).

Figure 5.19   Operational definitions for each metric.

Operational Definitions

Defining the Measure

<u>% Trailer Utilization</u>—A percentage of total trailer hours used per day by total trailer hours available per day. Quantitative, continuous measure, and ratio data.

Purpose

To document the use of trailer resources.

Clear way to measure the process

The data source is the Trailer Plan Log, which, when queried will produce the total trailer hours per day. The hours included are only the hours represented by the shipments completed by midnight. The hours available are calculated by 24 hours times the total trailers in the region. The data query will span 12 months prior to query.

Operational Definitions

Defining the Measure

<u>Daily Shipments</u>—Total shipments per day. Quantitative, discrete measure, and ratio data.

Purpose

To document trend of shipments by day within 12 months.

Clear way to measure the process

The data source is the Trailer Plan Log, which, when queried will produce the total daily shipments. The shipments included are only the shipments completed by midnight. The data query will span 12 months prior to query.

Figure 5.19 (continued).

Operational Definitions

Defining the Measure

% Empty—Calculated percentage of empty shipments by total shipments within one day. Quantitative, continuous measure, and ratio data.

Purpose

The goal is to examine the impact of using backhauls to improve trailer utilization.

Clear way to measure the process

The data source is the Trailer Plan Log, which, when queried will produce the total daily shipments and the total empty shipments by day. The data query will span 12 months prior to query.

Operational Definitions

Defining the Measure

Arrive On Schedule%—A calculated percentage of shipments that arrive on time by total shipments per day. Quantitative, continuous measure, and ratio data.

Purpose

To document how well the delivery of shipments meet the goal of arriving as planned.

Clear way to measure the process

The data source is the Trailer Plan Log, which, when queried will produce the total daily shipments and the total late AOS shipments by day (AOS has no tolerance, ETA is goal). 1-(late shipments/total) will produce the AOS%. The data query will span 12 months prior to query.

Figure 5.19   (continued).

Operational Definitions

Defining the Measure

Leave On Schedule%—A calculated percentage of shipments that leave on time by total shipments per day. Quantitative, continuous measure, and ratio data.

Purpose

To document how well the delivery of shipments meet the goal of leaving as planned.

Clear way to measure the process

The data source is the Trailer Plan Log, which, when queried will produce the total daily shipments and the total late LOS shipments by day (LOS has no tolerance, ETL is goal). 1-(late shipments/total) will produce the LOS%. The data query will span 12 months prior to query.

Operational Definitions

Defining the Measure

Dispatch Mean—A calculated average of dispatch time in minutes by day. Quantitative, continuous measure, and ratio data.

Purpose

To document the daily average dispatch time for trending and goal analysis.

Clear way to measure the process

The data source is the Trailer Plan Log, which, when queried will produce the dispatch time (Dispatch time— Request time) which will then be averaged by day. The data query will span 12 months prior to query.

Figure 5.19 (continued).

Operational Definitions

Defining the Measure

Dispatch Deviation Mean—A calculated average of dispatch time deviations from a set target (30 minutes) in minutes.Negative is early and positive is late. Quantitative, continuous measure, and ratio data.

Purpose

To document the deviation from a set target of 30 minutes.

Clear way to measure the process

The data source is the Trailer Plan Log, which, when queried will produce the deviation between the set target of 30 minutes and dispatch time, averaged by day. The data query will span 12 months prior to query.

Operational Definitions

Defining the Measure

Arrival Deviation Mean—A calculated average of arrival time deviations from ETA target in minutes. Negative is early and positive is late. Quantitative, continuous measure, and ratio data.

Purpose

To document the deviation from the target estimated time of arrival (ETA).

Clear way to measure the process

The data source is the Trailer Plan Log, which, when queried will produce the deviation between ETA and arrival time, averaged by day. The data query will span 12 months prior to query.

Figure 5.19   (continued).

Operational Definitions

Defining the Measure

<u>Departure Deviation Mean</u>—A calculated average of departure time deviations from ETL target in minutes. Negative is early and positive is late. Quantitative, continuous measure, and ratio data.

Purpose

To document the deviation from the target estimated time of departure, abbreviated as ETL.

Clear way to measure the process

The data source is the Trailer Plan Log, which, when queried will produce the deviation between ETL and departure time, averaged by day. The data query will span 12 months prior to query.

Operational Definitions

Defining the Measure

<u>% responded by question</u>—Percentage of the number of positive responses relative to survey question by total responses. Quantitative, continuous measure, and ratio data.

Purpose

To convert survey data into quantitative data relative to each question's subject.

Clear way to measure the process

The survey questions will be presented to the stakeholder groups, percent responded will be calculated overall and broken down by rating group.

Figure 5.19 **(continued).**

Operational Definitions

Defining the Measure

Live Unload process time—Total time to unload a trailer at a store. Quantitative, continuous measure, and ratio data.

Purpose

To establish a target time for unloading.

Clear way to measure the process

Three fully loaded trailers will be delivered to 10 stores where the trailers will be unloaded 3 different times. A stop watch will start when the door is opened by the driver and will stop when the trailer has been emptied. The data will be used to set a target time for Live Unload and can be used for a repeatability and reproducibility study.

Operational Definitions

Defining the Measure

Zero-inventory items per store—A daily total of merchandise that is at a zero quantity divided by the total number of stores. Quantitative, continuous measure, and ratio data.

Purpose

To document missed potential sales due to no product on the shelf from the process' voice.

Clear way to measure the process

The data source is from all stores' inventory at midnight each day. The data query will span 12 months prior to query.

Figure 5.19 (continued).

Operational Definitions

Defining the Measure

POS Empty Shelf per store—A daily total of survey results from customers who are reporting that they did not purchase an item due to an empty shelf per store. Quantitative, continuous measure, and ratio data.

Purpose

To document missed potential sales due to no product on the shelf from the customer's voice.

Clear way to measure the process

The data source is from all stores' POS survey and downloaded daily at midnight. The total is then divided by the total number of stores. The survey will span 2 weeks.

Operational Definitions

Defining the Measure

Existing SOP%—A percentage of formal SOPs in place by total SOPs possible. Quantitative, continuous measure, and ratio data.

Purpose

To document the relative amount of SOPs formally in place.

Clear way to measure the process

SOP audit of processes outlined by Six Sigma team relative to the process maps built for the measure phase. Check sheet method used to tally if a formal SOP was published and distributed to those affected.

Figure 5.19   (continued).

Operational Definitions

Defining the Measure

% Knowledge of Existing SOP—Percentage of the number of positive responses relative to survey question by total responses. Quantitative, continuous measure, and ratio data.

Purpose

To convert survey data into quantitative data relative to the knowledge of an SOP.

Clear way to measure the process

The survey question will be presented to the stakeholder groups, percent responded will be calculated overall and broken down by rating group. "Do you know the (CJ-Mart) operating procedures that affect you?"

Figure 5.19 (continued).

Create a Baseline

The team followed the data collection plan and gathered the data. The gathered data then needed to be assembled into a baseline document to establish where the process was currently at, as shown in Figure 5.20. Any changes to the process would be compared to the baseline for reference of change. Note that at this time there were a few metrics that relied on surveys that still needed to be conducted. Once they were completed, the baseline document was updated.

Metric	Baseline
Trailer Status	Not applicable. This metric is used in real time to drive the Trailer Status Error Rate.
Trailer Status Error Rate	Trailer Status Error Rate = 3.99%. 5% audit revealed 25 trailers incorrectly logged in the Trailer Plan Log.
%Trailer Utilization	Mean = 19.938%; StdDev = 3.543; Max = 28.964; Min = 11.905; UCL = 22.26; LCL = 17.61. Distribution is not normal. Trend is seasonal and follows Daily Shipments.
Daily Shipments	Mean = 19,064; StdDev = 3,351; Max = 26,889; Min = 11,751; UCL = 20,468; LCL = 17,660. Distribution is not normal. Trend is seasonal.
%Empty	Mean = 47.41%; StdDev = 1.438; Max = 49.977; Min = 43.314; UCL = 50.617; LCL = 47.094. Distribution is not normal. Trend shows special cause in the last few weeks of the year.
AOS%	Mean = 97.73%; StdDev = 1.851; Max = 100; Min = 93.202; UCL = 102.088; LCL = 93.373. Distribution is not normal.
LOS%	Mean = 97.833%; StdDev = 1.563; Max = 100; Min = 95.005; UCL = 102.83; LCL = 92.83. Distribution is not normal.
Dispatch Mean	Mean = 18.439; StdDev = 3.909; Max = 29.469; Min = 12.110; UCL = 27.34; LCL = 9.54. Distribution is not normal.
Dispatch Deviation Mean	Mean = −11.561; StdDev = 3.909; Max = −0.531; Min = −17.89; UCL = −2.66; LCL = −20.46. Distribution is not normal.
Arrival Deviation Mean	Mean = −28.993; StdDev = 12.502; Max = 7.047; Min = −45.484; UCL = −11.20; LCL = −46.79. Distribution is not normal.
Departure Deviation Mean	Mean = −34.638; StdDev = 11.441; Max = −6.497; Min = −55.329; UCL = −11.03; LCL = −58.24. Distribution is not normal.
% responded by question Topic: "Open communication of critical or jeopardy events"	Transportation: Driver Coord. Q1 "Within the last month, how often did drivers show up late at the destination dock without calling to alert you before their arrival?" 75% 1–10 times, 5% 11–20 times, 2% more than 20, 18% Never Q2 "Within the last month, how often did you notify a requestor of a late delivery or pickup before the trailer made it to the dock?" 14% 1–10 times, 0% 11–20 times, 0% more than 20, 86% Never

Figure 5.20   Baseline data for the process.

Metric	Baseline
% responded by question Topic: "Open communication of critical or jeopardy events"	Drivers: Driver Q3 "Within the last month, how often did you show up late at the destination dock without calling to alert a Driver Coordinator before your arrival?" 62% 1–10 times, 3% 11–20 times, 4% more than 20, 31% Never Late Q4 "Within the last month, how many times have you called a business critical resource and could not make contact within 1 hour?" 62% 1–5 times, 5% 6–10 times, 1% more than 10, 32% Never
% responded by question Topic: "Open communication of critical or jeopardy events"	Store Personnel: Store Manager, Receiving Dock Q5 "Within the last month, how often did a trailer show up late at the destination dock without anybody calling to alert you before its arrival?" 26% 1–5 times, 73% 6–10 times, 0% more than 10, 1% Never Late Q6 "Within the last month, how many times were you placed on hold waiting for a driver coordinator?" 48% 1–5 times, 3% 6–10 times, 1% more than 10, 15% Never, 33% N/A
% responded by question Topic: "Open communication of critical or jeopardy events"	Vendor: Operations Manager, Shipping Dock Q7 "Within the last month, how often did a trailer show up late at the destination dock without anybody calling to alert you before its arrival?" 36% 1–5 times, 1% 6–10 times, 1% more than 10, 62% Never Late Q8 "Within the last month, how many times were you placed on hold waiting for a driver coordinator?" 29% 1–5 times, 0% 6–10 times, 0% more than 10, 41% Never, 30% N/A

Figure 5.20   (continued).

Metric	Baseline
% responded by question Topic: "Open communication of critical or jeopardy events"	Warehouse: Managers, Shipping and Receiving Dock Q9 "Within the last month, how often did a trailer show up late at the destination dock without anybody calling to alert you before its arrival?" 33% 1–5 times, 1% 6–10 times, 0% more than 10, 66% Never Late Q10 "Within the last month, how many times were you placed on hold waiting for a driver coordinator?" 32% 1–5 times, 52% 6–10 times, 1% more than 10, 11% Never, 4% N/A
Departure Deviation Mean	Mean = −34.638; StdDev = 11.441; Max = −6.497; Min = −55.329; UCL = −11.03; LCL = −58.24. Distribution is not normal.
Live Unload Process Time	Mean = 63.422; StdDev = 10.876; Max = 85.0; Min = 45.0; UCL = 102.67; LCL = 24.18. Distribution is not normal.
Zero-inventory items per store	Mean = 16.372; StdDev = 11.558; Max = 49.4; Min = 8.7; UCL = 22.49; LCL = 10.26. Distribution is not normal.
POS Empty Shelf survey per store (2 weeks)	Mean = 2.5214; StdDev = 0.6841; Max = 4.0; Min = 1.9; UCL = 4.383; LCL = 0.66. Distribution is not normal.
Existing SOP%	Total SOPs possible = 10 Existing SOP% = 40%
% Knowledge of Existing SOP "Do you know the (CJMart) operating procedures that affect you?"	Transportation: Driver Coord. 　91% yes, 2% no, 7% not sure, 0% N/A Drivers: Driver 　31% yes, 14% no, 55% not sure, 0% N/A Store Personnel: Store Mgr., Rec. Dock 　83% yes, 6% no, 11% not sure, 0% N/A Vendor: Op. Mgr., Shipping Dock 　22% yes, 41% no, 32% not sure, 5% N/A Warehouse: Managers, Shipping and Receiving Dock 　95% yes, 1% no, 4% not sure, 0% N/A

Figure 5.20 (continued).

Define the Detailed Voice of the Customer (VOC)

The entire team had a role in gathering the VOC. The responsibility matrix and communication matrix provided the plan of what, when, who, and by whom. To gather the VOC, a series of three methods was used: interviews, focus groups, and surveys. Interviews were used for the smallest group, the transportation personnel. An overview of the customer needs is provided in Figure 5.21.

Interview Event

The first method the team used to gather the VOC was conducting interviews. Several of the customer/stakeholder groups were too large, so the team decided to survey these groups instead. The transportation personnel group—consisting of general managers, dispatch managers, and driver coordinators—was small enough

---

- Hosted interviews and focus groups to capture VOC
- Used affinity diagrams to sort and organize customer comments
- Gathered 32 different customer needs from four different groups
- Translated all needs into unofficial CTQs
- Built four surveys, each designed specifically for each group to gather qualitative data relative to the customer comments

---

Figure 5.21   Overview of customer needs.

to interview effectively. The key feedback and priorities from the transportation personnel included:

■ Prompt feedback from drivers when completing a delivery or pickup
■ Complete delivery or pickup requests
■ Requests presented within a reasonable window of opportunity
■ Standard and written processes
■ Training of stakeholders and customers on the standard processes

Given the size and location of the other customer groups, the team chose to use focus groups, in the form of town hall meetings, to gather their information and better define the VOC. The meetings were conducted live with the help of Web-based communications techniques. Four groups of customers/stakeholders were designated in the Define phase, which included:

■ Drivers
■ Store personnel: general managers and receiving personnel
■ Vendors: operational managers
■ Warehouse personnel: general managers, shipping and receiving personnel

A summary of the meeting notes is given in Figure 5.22.

The focus groups were to discuss the needs of each participant as they related to the trailer utilization process. The moderators also wanted to bring out any

- Team brainstormed what data to collect based on initial CTS
- Survey questions were written to help quantify the VOC
- Questions reviewed by Black Belt
- Met with Logistics personnel to refine the survey questions and to develop the process maps covered earlier in the presentation

Figure 5.22 Summary of meeting notes.

compliments or complaints about the current process. Brainstorming was the tool used to gather all of the comments given during each meeting. The comments were later used to build a survey to better determine if the needs were being met within each group. An overview of the focus-group information is given in Figure 5.23.

Focus groups in the form of town hall meetings were held for the customer/stakeholder groups:

- Drivers—CJMart employed
- Store—General Managers and Receiving Personnel
- Vendor—Operations Managers
- Warehouse—General Managers, Receiving and Shipping Personnel

Formal brainstorming sessions were held within each of the focus groups to generate a list of needs which will be used to build CTS characteristics and survey questions. Affinity diagrams were developed from the ideas.

Figure 5.23 Overview of the focus group information.

Brainstorm Needs

The focus groups were held for each customer/stake-holder group. The brainstorm lists for each are outlined here by group.

Drivers:
- Prompt replies from driver coordinators
- Dispatch correctly, right place, dock, and time
- Resources for emergency changes in travel plan
- No hold time when calling driver coordinators
- Correct contact information for destination site
- Quick turnaround when live unloading
- Realistic leave-on-schedule and arrive-on-schedule times

Store personnel—general managers and receiving personnel:
- Trailer needs to be here on time
- Correct documentation/packing list
- Easy procedure to get schedule updates
- Communication process to provide feedback to Logistics
- Notification when trailer will be late or shipment is in jeopardy

Vendor—operational managers:
- Easy method to request a pickup
- Scheduling that does not conflict with normal dock hours
- Provide an empty when a pickup request is made
- Trailers that are safe and secure

Warehouse personnel—general managers, shipping/ receiving personnel:

■ Arrive on schedule

■ Leave on schedule

■ Provide the correct and complete paperwork when dropping a load

■ Provide an empty trailer within an agreed time from time of request

■ Notify the drivers about their responsibility to check and secure loads leaving the dock

Affinity Diagrams

During the town halls, the moderators assisted the customers with organizing their comments into common areas of association. They formed affinity diagrams so that each focus group had its own organized set of comments, as shown in Figures 5.24–5.28.

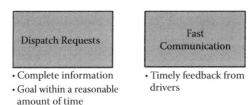

Figure 5.24   Transportation affinity diagram.

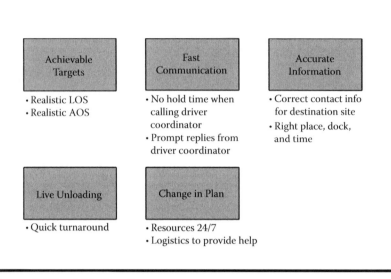

Figure 5.25 Affinity diagram.

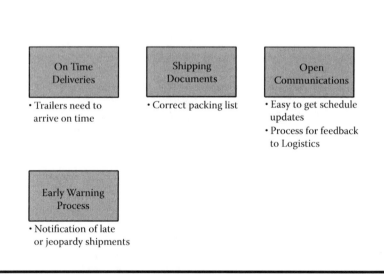

Figure 5.26 Store personnel affinity diagram.

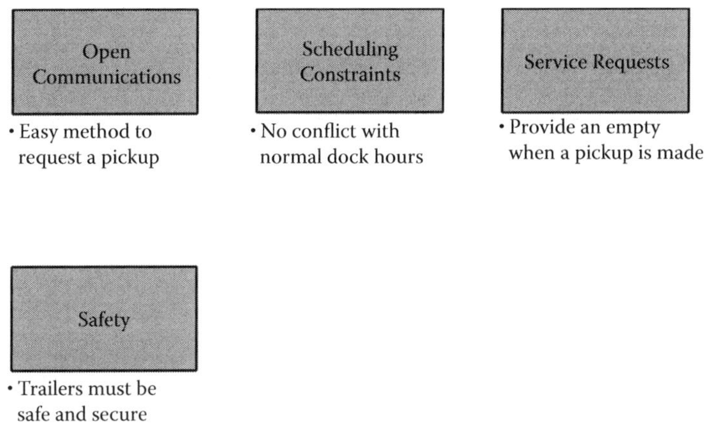

Open
Communications

• Easy method to
  request a pickup

Scheduling
Constraints

• No conflict with
  normal dock hours

Service Requests

• Provide an empty
  when a pickup is made

Safety

• Trailers must be
  safe and secure

Figure 5.27   Vendor affinity diagram.

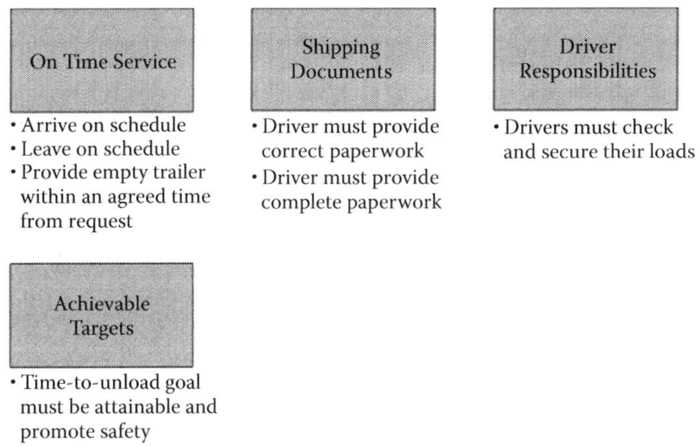

On Time Service

• Arrive on schedule
• Leave on schedule
• Provide empty trailer
  within an agreed time
  from request

Shipping
Documents

• Driver must provide
  correct paperwork
• Driver must provide
  complete paperwork

Driver
Responsibilities

• Drivers must check
  and secure their loads

Achievable
Targets

• Time-to-unload goal
  must be attainable and
  promote safety

Figure 5.28   Warehouse personnel affinity diagram.

Translate Needs to CTQ

The entire team gathered for a meeting to review the customer comments and then convert them into customer needs by discussing the key issues. Essentially, the team was translating the customer comments into the team's language. Sometimes the comments had multiple key issues, which resulted in more than one need from just one comment. The subject headings from the affinity diagrams were used to keep similar comments together. Some focus groups had the same or similar subject headings, which were then merged. Once the customer needs were written, these needs were then translated into critical-to-quality (CTQ) characteristics. Figures 5.29–5.43 show the translation at each stage.

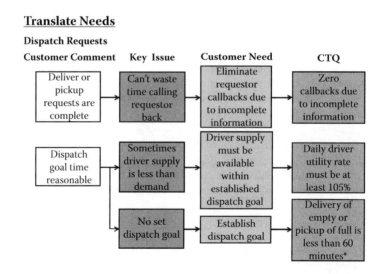

Figure 5.29   Dispatch requests translation into CTQ characteristics.

Translate Needs

Fast Communication

Customer Comment	Key Issue	Customer Need	CTQ

Timely feedback from drivers → Need up to date driver and trailer status → Driver to contact coordinator when entering staging zone → Contact to be made 30 minutes before docking

Driver to contact coordinator when travel plan changes → Contact to be made when change is more than 1 hour past AOS time

No hold time when calling driver coordinator → Driver coordinator staff capability → Establish staff loading standards based on historical demand → Maximum load is 20 calls per hour per coordinator

Prompt replies from driver coordinator → Driver coordinators use team service approach → Calls to be routed to first available

Figure 5.30 Fast communication translation into CTQ characteristics.

Translate Needs

Accurate Information

Customer Comment	Key Issue	Customer Need	CTQ

Correct contact information for destination site → Requestor profile database not kept current → Requestor contact information must be current → Coordinator must have requestor confirm contact info during request event

Right place, dock, and time → Incorrect information logged during request → Accurate request details → Coordinator to send request verification back to requestor

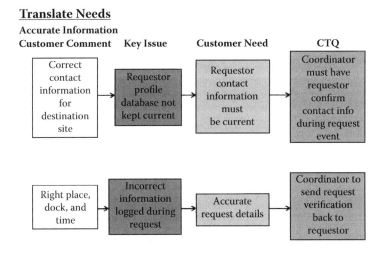

Figure 5.31 Accurate information translation into CTQ characteristics.

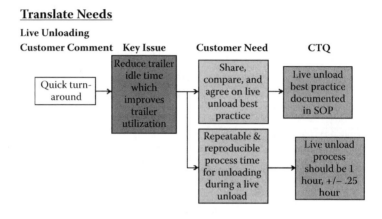

Figure 5.32   Live unloading translation into CTQ characteristics.

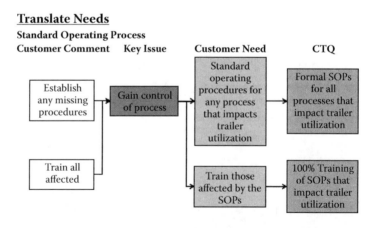

Figure 5.33   Standard operating process translation into CTQ characteristics.

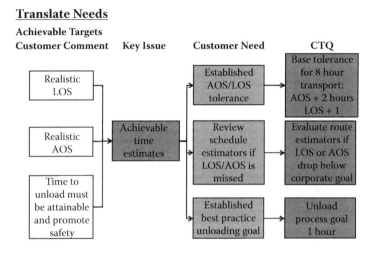

Figure 5.34   Achievable targets translated into CTQ characteristics.

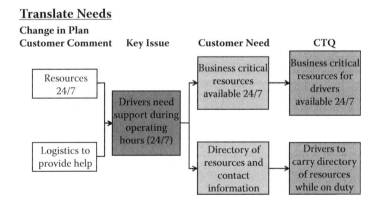

Figure 5.35   Change in plan translation into CTQ characteristics.

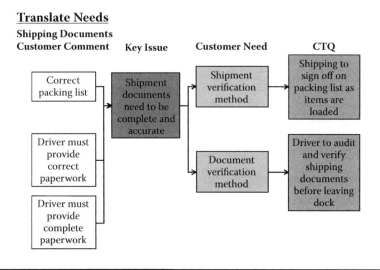

Figure 5.36 Shipping documents translated into CTQ characteristics.

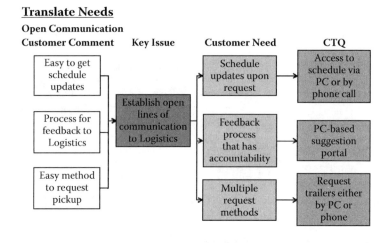

Figure 5.37 Open communication translated into CTQ characteristics.

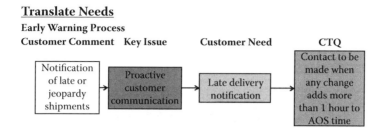

Figure 5.38 Early warning process translated into CTQ characteristics.

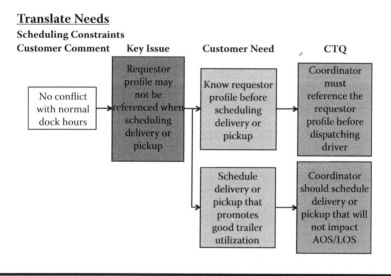

Figure 5.39 Scheduling constraints translated into CTQ characteristics.

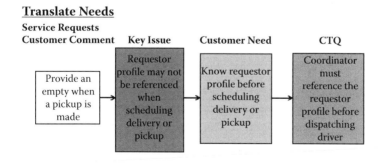

Figure 5.40 Service requests translated into CTQ characteristics.

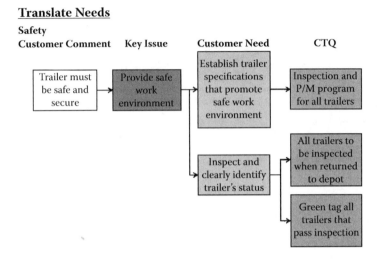

Figure 5.41   Safety needs translated into CTQ characteristics.

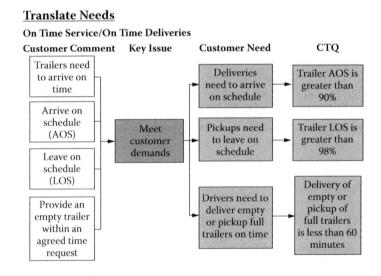

Figure 5.42   On time needs translated into CTQ characteristics.

Translate Needs

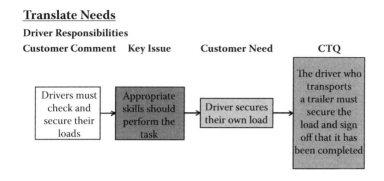

Figure 5.43   **Customer needs translated into CTQ characteristics.**

Survey Customers/Stakeholders

Now that the VOC of the customer had been heard and translated into a language that the team understood, the team needed to measure the VOC using a survey. The goal was to transfer the comments into quantitative data and define a process that can be repeated to verify change. The survey questions were built off the customer needs, which came from the customer comments. Five surveys were built to address each specific focus group. Some questions were common and spanned all five surveys. Some topics spanned multiple surveys, but the questions were asked specific to the respondent's role. The purpose of developing the surveys in this manner was to provide all views of the same fact that was in question.

The team had identified 32 customer needs and wanted to know the most important customer needs to focus on. So, they asked the customers within the survey to choose the 10 most important customer needs and then rank the top 3 of those 10. Some of the team members wanted the survey respondents to rank all 10, but the group decided asking for that would be too tedious and time consuming for the respondent. Besides, the team wanted to focus on the top needs first. Figures 5.44–5.48 provide the survey questions by group.

The team analyzed the survey results based on the selection of the top responses for each customer/stakeholder group. Once the survey results were tallied, the team built Pareto charts and noted key items from each survey group, as shown in Figures 5.49–5.68 (Data Figures 5.49–5.68). Some questions were originally part of the data collection plan, which was then updated with the results. The team planned to administer the survey again after changes were in place to validate or test that the changes improved the process.

Customer Needs Map

Now that that team had gathered the customer needs from the customer survey, they needed to organize the information and rank the needs. Jim Pulls reminded them to use a weighting scale of 9-3-1, when ranking the needs. The team gave a 9 if the survey group gave a number one rating, a 3 for number two rating, and a 1 for a number three rating of importance. The weights were then totaled for each need. The survey data for the ranked customer needs is shown in Figure 5.69 (Data Figure 5.69). For the Customer Needs map, the items were weighted, sorted in a descending order, and a percentage was noted for ranking.

Transportation Questions

Audience: Driver Coordinator

1. Within the last month, how often did you call a requestor back due to incomplete information?

   a) 1–10 times   b) 11–20 times   c) More than 20   d) Never

2. Within the last week, how often did you have more requests than drivers?

   a) 1–5 times   b) 6–10 times   c) More than 10   d) Never

3. Do you feel there needs to be a set goal for dispatch time (from request to dock)?

   a) Yes   b) No   c) Not sure   d) Does not apply

4. Within the last month, how often did drivers forget to call when entering the staging zone and just called once they were at their destination dock?

   a) 1–10 times   b) 11–20 times   c) More than 20   d) Never

5. Within the last month, how often did drivers show up late at the destination dock without calling to alert you before their arrival?

   a) 1–10 times   b) 11–20 times   c) More than 20   d) Never

6. Within the last month, how often did you provide incorrect contact information to drivers?

   a) 1–5 times   b) 6–10 times   c) More than 10   d) Never

7. Within the last month, how often did you log the incorrect request information?

   a) 1–5 times   b) 6–10 times   c) More than 10   d) Never

8. Within the last year, how often have you found that your suppliers and your customers are not following the standard procedures?

   a) 1–10 times   b) 11–20 times   c) More than 20   d) Always follow

9. Do you know the operating procedures that affect you?

   a) Yes   b) No   c) Not sure   d) Does not apply

10. Is there a formal training process for operating procedures?

    a) Yes   b) No   c) Not sure   d) Does not apply

11. Within the last month, how often has a driver called you requesting help for which you then had to forward them on to the correct resource?

    a) 1–5 times   b) 6–10 times   c) More than 10   d) Never

Figure 5.44 Transportation survey.

Transportation Questions

Audience: Driver Coordinator

12. Within the last month, how often did you provide schedule updates when somebody called requesting them?

    a) 1–10 times   b) 11–20 times   c) More than 20   d) Never

13. Within the last month, how often did you notify a requestor of a late delivery or pickup before the trailer made it to the dock?

    a) 1–10 times   b) 11–20 times   c) More than 20   d) Never

14. Within the last month, how often have you dispatched a delivery or pickup that became late because the requestor's docks were closed?

    a) 1–5 times   b) 6–10 times   c) More than 10   d) Never

15. Within the last month, how often did you forget to send an empty trailer when a vendor requested a pickup?

    a) 1–5 times   b) 6–10 times   c) More than 10   d) Never

16. Within the last year, have you had any reports of trailers which were considered to be an unsafe working environment?

    a) Yes   b) No   c) Not sure   d) Does not apply

17. Choose the top 10 customer needs relative to trailer utilization by placing an "X" on the line next to the item (mark only 10 items):

    _____ Eliminate requestor callbacks due to incomplete information

    _____ Driver supply must be available within established dispatch goal

    _____ Establish dispatch goal

    _____ Driver to contact Driver Coordinator when entering staging zone

    _____ Driver to contact Driver Coordinator when travel plan changes

    _____ Establish staff (Driver Coordinator) loading standards based on historical demand

    _____ Driver Coordinators use team service approach to help cover call load

    _____ Requestor contact information must be current

    _____ Accurate request details

    _____ Share, compare, and agree on Live Unload best practice

    _____ Repeatable and reproducible process time for unloading during a Live Unload

Figure 5.44 **(continued).**

Transportation Questions

Audience: Driver Coordinator

_____ Standard Operating Procedures for any process that impacts trailer utilization

_____ Train those affected by trailer utilization Standard Operating Procedures

_____ Establish Arrive On Schedule (AOS) and Leave On Schedule (LOS) tolerance

_____ Review schedule estimators if AOS or LOS is missed

_____ Establish unloading goal based on best practice

_____ Business critical resources available for drivers 24/7

_____ Drivers to have a directory of resources with contact information

_____ Establish a shipment verification method

_____ Establish a shipment document verification method

_____ Logistics to provide schedule updates upon request

_____ Logistics to establish a feedback process that has accountability

_____ Logistics to offer multiple trailer delivery or pickup request methods

_____ Driver Coordinator to provide a late delivery notification

_____ Driver Coordinator to review requestor profile before scheduling delivery or pickup

_____ Driver Coordinator to schedule delivery or pickup that promotes good trailer utilization

_____ Logistics to establish trailer specifications which promote a safe work environment

_____ Trailer inspection date and status need to be clearly documented on trailer

_____ Deliveries need to arrive on schedule

_____ Pickups need to leave on schedule

_____ Drivers need to secure their own loads

18. Do you understand all of the customer needs listed in question 17? If not please highlight those that would need explanation.

    a) Yes   b) No   c) Not sure

19. Do you have customer needs that were not listed in question 17? If so please, write your customer needs on the back of this sheet.

    a) Yes   b) No   c) Not sure

Figure 5.44   (continued).

Driver Questions

Audience: Driver

1. Do you feel there needs to be a set goal for dispatch time (from request to dock)?

   a) Yes   b) No   c) Not sure   d) Does not apply

2. Within the last month, how often did you forget to call when entering the staging zone and just called once you were at the destination dock?

   a) 1–5 times   b) 6–10 times   c) More than 10   d) Never

3. Within the last month, how often did you show up late at the destination dock without calling to alert a Driver Coordinator before your arrival?

   a) 1–10 times   b) 11–20 times   c) More than 20   d) Never

4. Within the last month, how many times were you placed on hold waiting for a driver coordinator?

   a) 1–5 times   b) 6–10 times   c) More than 10   d) Never

5. Within the last month, how often were you given the incorrect contact information for the destination site?

   a) 1–5 times   b) 6–10 times   c) More than 10   d) Never

6. Within the last month, how often did you wait more than an hour (time from dock to drive away) for a live unload process to complete?

   a) 1–5 times   b) 6–10 times   c) More than 10   d) Never

7. Do you know the operating procedures that affect you?

   a) Yes   b) No   c) Not sure   d) Does not apply

8. Is there a formal training process for operating procedures?

   a) Yes   b) No   c) Not sure   d) Does not apply

9. Within the last month, how many times have you arrived late by more than 2 hours with a delivery?

   a) 1–5 times   b) 6–10 times   c) More than 10   d) Never

10. Within the last month, how many times have you departed late by more than 1 hour with a pickup?

    a) 1–5 times   b) 6–10 times   c) More than 10   d) Never

11. Are there particular routes that you always seem to arrive more than 2 hours late?

    a) Yes   b) No   c) Not sure   d) Does not apply

Figure 5.45 Driver survey.

Driver Questions

Audience: Driver

12. Within the last month, how many times have you called a business critical resource and could not make contact within 1 hour?

a) 1–5 times   b) 6–10 times   c) More than 10   d) Never

13. Within the last month, how often have you called a Driver Coordinator requesting help for which you then had to be forwarded on to the correct resource?

a) 1–5 times   b) 6–10 times   c) More than 10   d) Never

14. Within the last month, how often have you been given a packet of shipping documents that were incorrect?

a) 1–5 times   b) 6–10 times   c) More than 10   d) Never

15. Within the last month, how often have you been given a packet of shipping documents that were incomplete?

a) 1–5 times   b) 6–10 times   c) More than 10   d) Never

16. Within the last month, how often have arrived at a destination site to find the docks were closed?

a) 1–5 times   b) 6–10 times   c) More than 10   d) Never

17. Do you always check and secure your own load before leaving the dock?

a) Yes   b) No   c) Not my job   d) Does not apply

18. Choose the top 10 customer needs relative to trailer utilization by placing an "X" on the line next to the item (mark only 10 items).
Then rank the top 3 of your chosen 10 with 1 being the most important:

STANDARD LIST OF CUSTOMER NEEDS

19. Do you understand all of the customer needs listed in question 18? If not please highlight those that would need explanation.

a) Yes   b) No   c) Not sure

20. Do you have customer needs that were not listed in question 18? If so please, write your customer needs on the back of this sheet.

a) Yes   b) No   c) Not sure

Figure 5.45   (continued).

Store Personnel Questions

Audience: Store Mgr., Receiving Dock Personnel

1. Within the last month, how often did a trailer show up late at your dock without anybody calling to alert you before its arrival?

   a) 1–5 times   b) 6–10 times   c) More than 10   d) Never

2. Within the last month, how many times were you placed on hold waiting for a Driver Coordinator?

   a) 1–5 times   b) 6–10 times   c) More than 10   d) Never   e) Does not apply

3. Within the last month, how often did you take more than an hour (time from dock to drive away) to complete a live unload process?

   a) 1–5 times   b) 6–10 times   c) More than 10   d) Never

4. Do you know the operating procedures that affect you?

   a) Yes   b) No   c) Not sure   d) Does not apply

5. Is there a formal training process for operating procedures?

   a) Yes   b) No   c) Not sure   d) Does not apply

6. Within the last month, how often did a driver arrive with incorrect shipping documents?

   a) 1–5 times   b) 6–10 times   c) More than 10   d) Never

7. Within the last month, how often did a driver arrive with incomplete shipping documents?

   a) 1–5 times   b) 6–10 times   c) More than 10   d) Never

8. Within the last month, how often did you call to request a schedule update for a trailer arrival time?

   a) 1–5 times   b) 6–10 times   c) More than 10   d) Never

9. Choose the top 10 customer needs relative to trailer utilization by placing an "X" on the line next to the item (mark only 10 items).

   Then rank the top 3 of your chosen 10 with 1 being the most important:

   STANDARD LIST OF CUSTOMER NEEDS

10. Do you understand all of the customer needs listed in question 9? If not please highlight those that would need explanation.

    a) Yes   b) No   c) Not sure

11. Do you have customer needs that were not listed in question 9? If so please, write your customer needs on the back of this sheet.

    a) Yes   b) No   c) Not sure

Figure 5.46 Store personnel survey.

Vendor Questions

Audience: Operations Mgr., Shipping Mgr., Dock Personnel

1. Do you feel there needs to be a set goal for dispatch time (from request to dock)?

   a) Yes   b) No   c) Not sure   d) Does not apply

2. Within the last month, how often did a trailer show up late at your dock without anybody calling to alert you before its arrival?

   a) 1–5 times   b) 6–10 times   c) More than 10   d) Never

3. Within the last month, how many times were you placed on hold waiting for a driver coordinator?

   a) 1–5 times   b) 6–10 times   c) More than 10   d) Never   e) Does not apply

4. Do you know where to find CJ-Mart operating procedures that affect you?

   a) Yes   b) No   c) Not sure   d) Does not apply

5. Do you know of a formal CJ-Mart training process for operating procedures?

   a) Yes   b) No   c) Not sure   d) Does not apply

6. Do you have a formal shipment verification method in place that assures the shipping documents are complete and correct?

   a) Yes   b) No   c) Not sure   d) Does not apply

7. Within the last month, how often did you call to request a schedule update for a trailer arrival time?

   a) 1–5 times   b) 6–10 times   c) More than 10   d) Never

8. What is your preferred method of requesting trailer deliveries or pickups?

   a) PC   b) Phone   c) FAX   d) Other

9. Within the last month, how often has a delivery or pickup arrived at your site when the docks were closed?

   a) 1–5 times   b) 6–10 times   c) More than 10   d) Never

10. Within the last month, how often did you not receive an empty trailer when you requested a pickup?

    a) 1–5 times   b) 6–10 times   c) More than 10   d) Never

11. Within the last year, have often have you received a trailer you considered to be an unsafe working environment?

    a) 1–5 times   b) 6–10 times   c) More than 10   d) Never

Figure 5.47   Vendor survey.

Vendor Questions

Audience: Operations Mgr., Shipping Mgr., Dock Personnel

12. Within the last year, have you reported your concern of the trailers that you considered to be an unsafe working environment?

   a) Yes   b) No   c) Not sure   d) Does not apply

13. Choose the top 10 customer needs relative to trailer utilization by placing an "X" on the line next to the item (mark only 10 items).

   Then rank the top 3 of your chosen 10 with 1 being the most important:

   STANDARD LIST OF CUSTOMER NEEDS

14. Do you understand all of the customer needs listed in question 13? If not please highlight those that would need explanation.

   a) Yes   b) No   c) Not sure

15. Do you have customer needs that were not listed in question 13? If so please, write your customer needs on the back of this sheet.

   a) Yes   b) No   c) Not sure

Figure 5.47   (continued).

Warehouse Questions

Audience: Warehouse Mgr., Receiving Mgr., Shipping Mgr., Dock Personnel

1. Do you feel there needs to be a set goal for dispatch time (from request to dock)?

   a) Yes   b) No   c) Not sure   d) Does not apply

2. Within the last month, how often did a trailer show up late at your dock without anybody calling to alert you before its arrival?

   a) 1–5 times   b) 6–10 times   c) More than 10   d) Never

3. Within the last month, how many times were you placed on hold waiting for a driver coordinator?

   a) 1–5 times   b) 6–10 times   c) More than 10   d) Never   e) Does not apply

Figure 5.48   Warehouse survey.

Warehouse Questions

Audience: Warehouse Mgr., Receiving Mgr., Shipping Mgr., Dock Personnel

4. Do you know where to find operating procedures that affect you?

   a) Yes   b) No   c) Not sure   d) Does not apply

5. Is there a formal training process for operating procedures?

   a) Yes   b) No   c) Not sure   d) Does not apply

6. Within the last month, how often did a driver arrive with incorrect shipping documents?

   a) 1–5 times   b) 6–10 times   c) More than 10   d) Never

7. Within the last month, how often did a driver arrive with incomplete shipping documents?

   a) 1–5 times   b) 6–10 times   c) More than 10   d) Never

8. Within the last month, how often did you call to request a schedule update for a trailer arrival time?

   a) 1–5 times   b) 6–10 times   c) More than 10   d) Never

9. What is your preferred method of requesting trailer deliveries or pickups?

   a) PC   b) Phone   c) FAX   d) Other

10. Does the driver always check and secure their own load before leaving the dock?

    a) Yes   b) No   c) Not driver's job   d) Does not apply

11. Choose the top 10 customer needs relative to trailer utilization by placing an "X" on the line next to the item (mark only 10 items).

    Then rank the top 3 of your chosen 10 with 1 being the most important:

    STANDARD LIST OF CUSTOMER NEEDS

12. Do you understand all of the customer needs listed in question 11? If not please highlight those that would need explanation.

    a) Yes   b) No   c) Not sure

13. Do you have customer needs that were not listed in question 11? If so please, write your customer needs on the back of this sheet.

    a) Yes   b) No   c) Not sure

Figure 5.48   (continued).

- Audience
  - Driver Coordinator with at least 1 year of service
  - 44 of 72 participated in the survey (61% response rate)
- Top 3 Needs that Influence Trailer Utilization
  - Deliveries need to arrive on schedule
  - Establish a dispatch goal
  - Establish AOS and LOS tolerance
- Interesting Findings
  - 84% had to call request or back 1–10 times per month
  - 61% had more requests than drivers 6–10 times per week
  - 77% had logged incorrect request info 1–5 times per month

Figure 5.49   Transportation personnel survey overview.

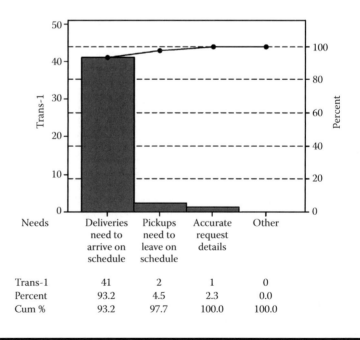

	Deliveries need to arrive on schedule	Pickups need to leave on schedule	Accurate request details	Other
Trans-1	41	2	1	0
Percent	93.2	4.5	2.3	0.0
Cum %	93.2	97.7	100.0	100.0

Figure 5.50   Pareto chart of #1 transportation needs.

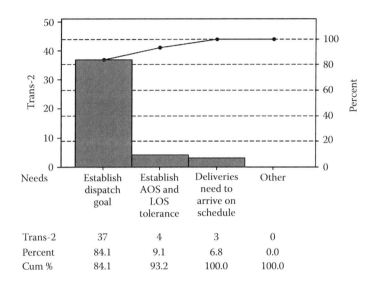

Needs	Establish dispatch goal	Establish AOS and LOS tolerance	Deliveries need to arrive on schedule	Other
Trans-2	37	4	3	0
Percent	84.1	9.1	6.8	0.0
Cum %	84.1	93.2	100.0	100.0

Figure 5.51   Pareto chart of #2 transportation needs.

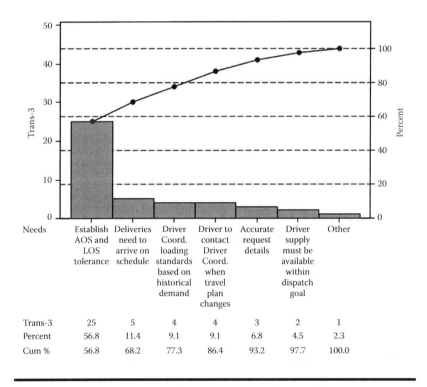

Needs	Establish AOS and LOS tolerance	Deliveries need to arrive on schedule	Driver Coord. loading standards based on historical demand	Driver to contact Driver Coord. when travel plan changes	Accurate request details	Driver supply must be available within dispatch goal	Other
Trans-3	25	5	4	4	3	2	1
Percent	56.8	11.4	9.1	9.1	6.8	4.5	2.3
Cum %	56.8	68.2	77.3	86.4	93.2	97.7	100.0

Figure 5.52   Pareto chart of #3 transportation needs.

- Audience
  - Drivers with at least 1 year of service
  - 325 of 900 participated in the survey (36% response rate)
- Top 3 Needs that Influence Trailer Utilization
  - Pickups need to leave on schedule
  - Establish AOS and LOS tolerance
  - Establish dispatch goal
- Interesting Findings
  - 62% were late arriving and did not alert Driver Coord. before docking 1–10 times per month
  - 85% waited more than 1 hour for live unload 6–10 times per month
  - 24% were late by more than 2 hours 1–5 times per month

Figure 5.53

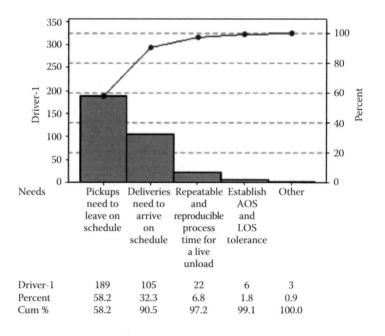

Needs	Pickups need to leave on schedule	Deliveries need to arrive on schedule	Repeatable and reproducible process time for a live unload	Establish AOS and LOS tolerance	Other
Driver-1	189	105	22	6	3
Percent	58.2	32.3	6.8	1.8	0.9
Cum %	58.2	90.5	97.2	99.1	100.0

Figure 5.54   Pareto chart of #1 driver needs.

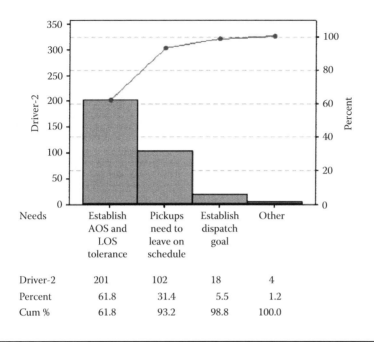

Figure 5.55   Pareto chart of #2 driver needs.

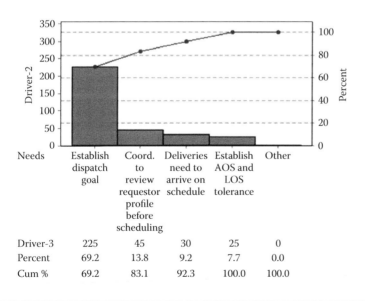

Figure 5.56   Pareto chart of #3 driver needs.

- Audience
    - Store Manager and Receiving Dock Personnel with at least 1 year of service
    - 422 of 1,260 participated in the survey (33% response rate)
- Top 3 Needs that Influence Trailer Utilization
    - Deliveries need to be on a schedule
    - Repeatable and reproducible process time for a live unload
    - Review schedule estimators if AOS or LOS is missed
- Interesting Findings
    - 73% reported a trailer was late without anybody contacting them 6–10 times per month
    - 73% reported a live unload greater than 1 hour 1–5 times per month

Figure 5.57

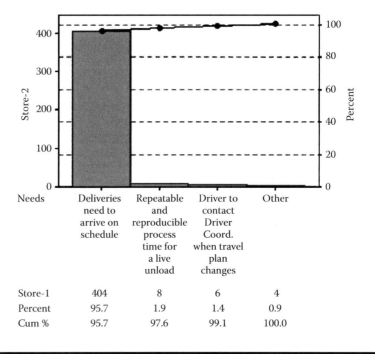

Needs	Deliveries need to arrive on schedule	Repeatable and reproducible process time for a live unload	Driver to contact Driver Coord. when travel plan changes	Other
Store-1	404	8	6	4
Percent	95.7	1.9	1.4	0.9
Cum %	95.7	97.6	99.1	100.0

Figure 5.58   Pareto chart of #1 store needs.

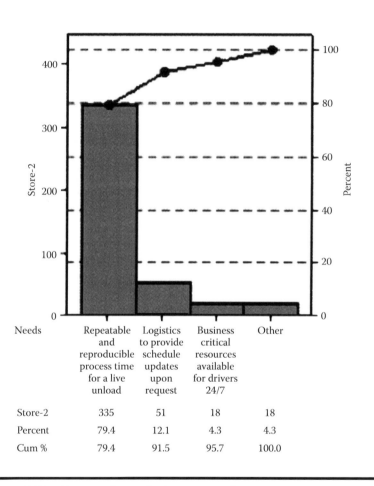

Needs	Repeatable and reproducible process time for a live unload	Logistics to provide schedule updates upon request	Business critical resources available for drivers 24/7	Other
Store-2	335	51	18	18
Percent	79.4	12.1	4.3	4.3
Cum %	79.4	91.5	95.7	100.0

Figure 5.59   Pareto chart of #2 store needs.

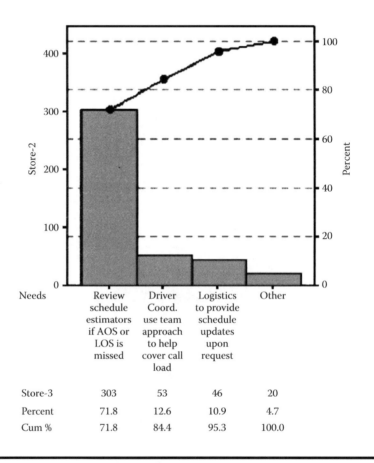

Needs	Review schedule estimators if AOS or LOS is missed	Driver Coord. use team approach to help cover call load	Logistics to provide schedule updates upon request	Other
Store-3	303	53	46	20
Percent	71.8	12.6	10.9	4.7
Cum %	71.8	84.4	95.3	100.0

Figure 5.60   Pareto chart of #3 store needs.

- ▪ Audience
  - – Operations Managers, Shipping Managers, and Dock Personnel with at least 2 year of service
  - – 278 of 888 participated in the survey (31% response rate)
- ▪ Top 3 Needs that Influence Trailer Utilization
  - – Deliveries need to arrive on schedule
  - – Accurate request details
  - – Driver to contact Driver Coordinator when travel plans change
- ▪ Interesting Findings
  - – 36% reported a trailer was late without anybody contacting them 1–5 times per month
  - – 52% had trailers arrive at their docks when they were closed 6–10 times per month

Figure 5.61   Vendor survey overview.

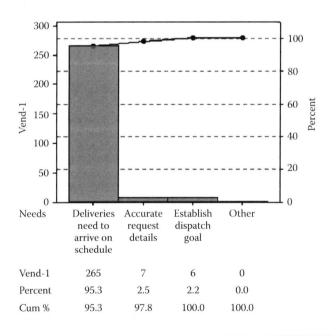

	Deliveries need to arrive on schedule	Accurate request details	Establish dispatch goal	Other
Vend-1	265	7	6	0
Percent	95.3	2.5	2.2	0.0
Cum %	95.3	97.8	100.0	100.0

Figure 5.62   Pareto chart of #1 vendor needs.

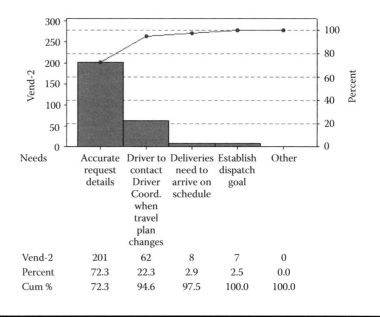

Needs	Accurate request details	Driver to contact Driver Coord. when travel plan changes	Deliveries need to arrive on schedule	Establish dispatch goal	Other
Vend-2	201	62	8	7	0
Percent	72.3	22.3	2.9	2.5	0.0
Cum %	72.3	94.6	97.5	100.0	100.0

Figure 5.63   Pareto chart of #2 vendor needs.

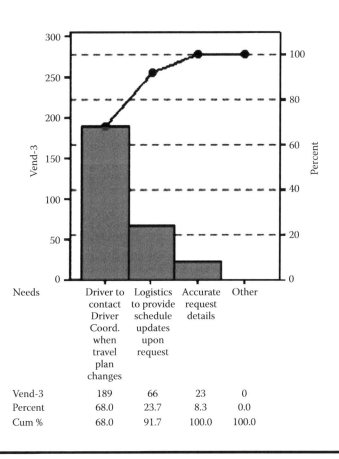

Needs	Driver to contact Driver Coord. when travel plan changes	Logistics to provide schedule updates upon request	Accurate request details	Other
Vend-3	189	66	23	0
Percent	68.0	23.7	8.3	0.0
Cum %	68.0	91.7	100.0	100.0

Figure 5.64   Pareto chart of #3 vendor needs.

- Audience
  - Warehouse Managers, Receiving Managers, Shipping Managers, and Dock Personnel with at least 1 year of service
  - 413 of 1,122 participated in the survey (36% response rate)
- Top 3 Needs that Influence Trailer Utilization
  - Deliveries need to arrive on schedule
  - SOPs for any process that impacts trailer utilization
  - Driver supply must be available within established dispatch goal
- Interesting Findings
  - 97% feel there needs to be an established dispatch goal
  - 75% had trailers arrive with incorrect shipping documents 1–5 times per month

Figure 5.65   Warehouse survey overview.

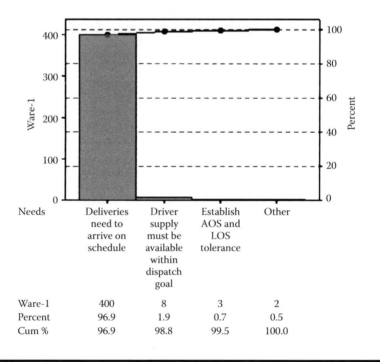

Needs	Deliveries need to arrive on schedule	Driver supply must be available within dispatch goal	Establish AOS and LOS tolerance	Other
Ware-1	400	8	3	2
Percent	96.9	1.9	0.7	0.5
Cum %	96.9	98.8	99.5	100.0

Figure 5.66   Pareto chart of #1 warehouse needs.

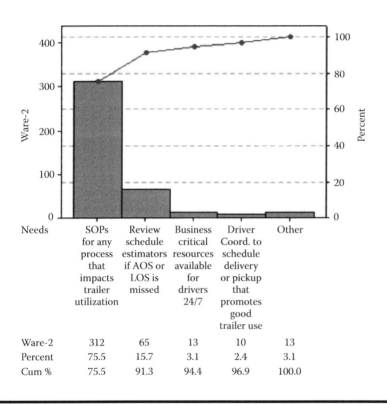

Needs	SOPs for any process that impacts trailer utilization	Review schedule estimators if AOS or LOS is missed	Business critical resources available for drivers 24/7	Driver Coord. to schedule delivery or pickup that promotes good trailer use	Other
Ware-2	312	65	13	10	13
Percent	75.5	15.7	3.1	2.4	3.1
Cum %	75.5	91.3	94.4	96.9	100.0

Figure 5.67 Pareto chart of #2 warehouse needs.

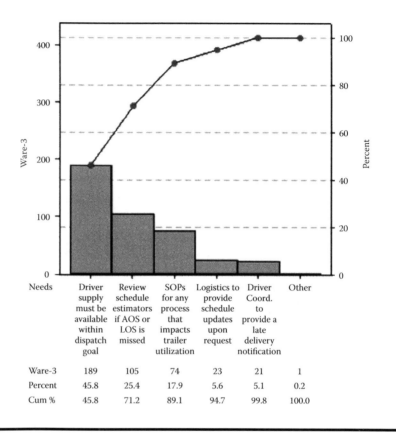

Needs	Driver supply must be available within dispatch goal	Review schedule estimators if AOS or LOS is missed	SOPs for any process that impacts trailer utilization	Logistics to provide schedule updates upon request	Driver Coord. to provide a late delivery notification	Other
Ware-3	189	105	74	23	21	1
Percent	45.8	25.4	17.9	5.6	5.1	0.2
Cum %	45.8	71.2	89.1	94.7	99.8	100.0

Figure 5.68   Pareto chart of #3 warehouse needs.

Quality Function Deployment (QFD)

A QFD matrix was used to check for gaps between the VOC and the current process and to determine which metrics to explore. Anita expressed her liking of this tool. She had seen its benefit during her first Black Belt project. She explained that the team now knew the VOC, but did the process address it? The customer requirement used was the list of customer needs from the survey, and the importance was the weighted score. The technical requirements came directly from the translation of customer need to CTQ, as shown in Figure 5.70. There was much debate about the weighted relationship

Customer Need	Trans	Driver	Store	Vendor	Ware
Establish AOS and LOS tolerance	3rd	2nd			
Repeatable & reproducible process time for live unload			2nd		
Establish a dispatch goal	2nd	3rd			
Pickups need to leave on schedule		1st			
Accurate request details				2nd	
SOP for any process that impacts trailer utilization					2nd
Deliveries need to arrive on schedule	1st		1st	1st	1st
Driver to contact Driver Coordinator when travel plan changes				3rd	
Driver supply must be available within established dispatch goal					3rd
Review schedule estimators if AOS or LOS is missed			3rd		

Figure 5.69   Ranked customer needs from survey data.

between each customer requirement and the technical requirements given. Also, some CTQs were stated with a metric target, but some did not exist in the current process.

Define the Voice of the Process (VOP) and Current Performance

Now that the process and the VOC had been defined, it was time to investigate the voice of the process (VOP) and its current performance. The team decided from the beginning of this phase to build a VOP matrix before

Legend

Symbol	Meaning	Value
⊙	Strong Relationship	9
○	Moderate Relationship	3
◣	Weak Relationship	1
⧺	Strong Positive Correlation	
+	Positive Correlation	
−	Negative Correlation	
▼	Strong Negative Correlation	
▶	Objective Is To Minimize	
◀	Objective Is To Maximize	
×	Objective Is To Hit Target	

Direction of Improvement: Minimize (▼), Maximize (▲), or Target (x)

Technical Requirements (a.k.a. "Hows")

Column #	Row #	Weight / Importance	Customer Requirements (a.k.a. "Whats")	1 Track AOS Metric	2 Track LOS Metric	3 Deliver or pickup of trailer is within time limit	4 AOS - base tolerance for 8 hour transport	5 LOS - base tolerance for 8 hour transport	6 Requestor verification	7 Live unload process standard (+/- 0.25 hr)	8 SOP's for all trailer utilization processes	9 Contact when change is more than 1 hour past AOS	10 Evaluate route estimates if LOS or AOS is below standard	11 Daily driver utility rate standard
	1	36.0	Deliveries need to arrive on schedule	⊙		◣	○				◣	⊙	◣	
	2	9.0	Pickups need to leave on schedule	○	⊙	◣					◣		◣	
	3	4.0	Establish a dispatch goal			⊙					◣			
	4	4.0	Establish AOS and LOS tolerance				⊙	⊙			◣			
	5	3.0	Accurate request details						⊙		◣			
	6	3.0	Repeatable and reproducible process time for live unload							⊙	⊙			
	7	3.0	SOP for any process that impacts trailer utilization								◣			⊙
	8	1.0	Driver supply must be available within dispatch goal								◣			
	9	1.0	Driver to contact coordinator when travel plan changes								◣	⊙		
	10	1.0	Review schedule estimators if AOS or LOS is missed										⊙	
			Metric Unit	%	%	min	hr	hr	%	hr	%	%	%	%
			Value	90	98	60	2	1	100	1	100	100	100	105
			Absolute Weight	325	82	81	144	63	63	72	89	117	54	36
			Relative Weight	1	5	6	2	8	8	7	4	3	9	10

Figure 5.70 Voice of the process matrix.

continuing further with the VOP. They brought together key information from different documents into one sheet to make reference easier. The CTS and metric data were brought in from the data-collection plan. This information was matched with its respective operational definition (which the team condensed). The team then charted the factors that impacted the metric and documented the current target. This sheet became handy, because each team member had the definition, target, impacting factors, and CTS relationship for each metric in one place, as shown in Figure 5.71.

Benchmarking

Simone Fillbert and Joe Thompson took on the role of researching other industry leaders to find out more about what made them leaders. This information was then organized, summarized, and placed in a benchmarking matrix, as shown in Figure 5.72. The goal was not just to look at other leaders in retail supply chain management. They picked leaders of quality processes and wanted to better understand how each company or business did it so well. In the end, they found that businesses in a competitive market were consistent in their processes while offering what the customer really wanted.

Check Sheets

The team needed to collect some data via audits of real events, so they decided to use check sheets to gather the data for the trailer status audit and the attribute gauge repeatability and reproducibility (R&R) for Trailer Log

CTS	Factors	Operational Definition	Metric	Target
Up-to-date trailer status	• Incorrect logging of trailer	Calculated percentage of the incorrect trailer status tally by the total trailers audited. Trailer status data is extracted from Trailer Plan Log in real-time during the audit. A random list of 5% of the trailers will be used to choose the trailers to audit.	Trailer Status Error Rate	0%
Optimized trailer dispatch plan	• Daily shipments • Trailer total available	Calculated percentage of total trailer hours used per day by total trailer hours available per day. The data source is the Trailer Plan Log.	% Trailer Utilization	Not defined
	• Vendor Requests • Warehouse Requests	Total shipments per day. The data source is the Trailer Plan Log.	Daily Shipments	Not defined
	• Backhaul quantity	Calculated percentage of empty shipments by total shipments within one day. The data source is the Trailer Plan Log.	%Empty	Not defined
Optimized trailer dispatch plan	• Route estimate (ETA) • LOS% • Timing of the driver's call and the logging	Calculated percentage of shipments that arrive on time by total shipments per day. The data source is the Trailer Plan Log, which, when queried will produce the total daily shipments and the total late AOS shipments by day (AOS has no tolerance, ETA is goal). 1-(late shipments/total will produce the AOS%).	AOS%	100%
	• Driver Coordinator's decision	Calculated percentage of shipments that leave on time by total shipments per day. The data source is the Trailer Plan Log, which, when queried will produce the total daily shipments and the total late LOS shipments by day (LOS has no tolerance. ETL is goal).1-(late shipments/total) will produce the LOS%.	LOS%	100%
	• Driver availability • Coordinator's work load	Calculated average of dispatch time in minutes by day. The data source is the Trailer Plan Log, which, when queried will produce the dispatch time (Dispatch time minus Request time) which will then be averaged by day.	Dispatch Mean	Not defined

Figure 5.71 Voice of the process matrix.

CTS	Factors	Operational Definition	Metric	Target
Optimized trailer dispatch plan	• Unofficial target of 30 minutes • Same as dispatch mean	Calculated average of dispatch time deviations from a set target (30 minutes) in minutes. Negative is early and positive is late. The data source is the Trailer Plan Log, which, when queried will produce the deviation between the set target of 30 minutes and dispatch time, averaged by day.	Dispatch Deviation Mean	Not defined
	• Same as AOS%	Calculated average of arrival time deviations from ETA target in minutes. Negative is early and positive is late. The data source is the Trailer Plan Log, which, when queried will produce the deviation between ETA and Arrival time, averaged by day.	Arrival Deviation Mean	Not defined
	• Same as LOS%	Calculated average of departure time deviations from ETL target in minutes. Negative is early and positive is late. The data source is the Trailer Plan Log, which, when queried will produce the deviation between ETL and Departure time, averaged by day.	Departure Deviation Mean	Not defined.
Open communication of critical or jeopardy events		Transportation: Driver Coord. Q1 "Within the last month, how often did drivers show up late at the destination dock without calling to alert you before their arrival?" Q2 "Within the last month, how often did you notify a requestor of a late delivery or pickup before the trailer made it to the dock?" Drivers: Driver Q3 "Within the last month, how often did you show up late at the destination dock without calling to alert a Driver Coordinator before your arrival?" Q4 "Within the last month, how many times have you called a business critical resource and could not make contact within 1 hour?"	% responded by question	Q1 100% Never Q2 100% Never Q3 100% Never Late Q4 100% Never

Figure 5.71 (continued).

CTS	Factors	Operational Definition	Metric	Target
Open communication of critical or jeopardy events		Store Personnel: Store Managers. Receiving Dock		
		Q5 "Within the last month, how often did a trailer show up late at the destination dock without anybody calling to alert you before its arrival?"		Q5 100% Never Late
		Q6 "Within the last month, how many times were you placed on hold waiting for a driver coordinator?"		Q6 100% Never
		Vendor: Operations Manager. Shipping Dock	% responded by question	
		Q7 "Within the last month, how often did a trailer show up late at the destination dock without anybody calling to alert you before its arrival?"		Q7 100% Never Late
		Q8 "Within the last month, how many times were you placed on hold waiting for a driver coordinator?"		Q8 100% Never
		Warehouse: Managers. Shipping & Receiving Dock		
		Q9 "Within the last month, how often did a trailer show up late at the destination dock without anybody calling to alert you before its arrival?"		Q9 100% Never Late
		Q10 "Within the last month, how many times were you placed on hold waiting for a driver coordinator?"		Q10 100% Never
Realistic process time estimates and expectations	• Best practice • Equipment • Load type	Total time to unload a trailer at a store. Three fully loaded trailers will be delivered to 10 stores where the trailers will be unloaded 3 different times. A stop watch will start when the door is opened by the driver and will stop when the trailer has been emptied.	Live Unload Process Time	60 minutes
Meet store customers' demands	• Unpredicted demand • Change Vendor supply	Daily total of merchandise that is at a zero inventory divided by the total number of stores. The data source is from all stores' inventory at midnight each day.	Zero Inventory Items per Store	

Figure 5.71   (continued).

CTS	Factors	Operational Definition	Metric	Target
Meet store customers' demands	• Unpredicted demand change • Vendor supply	Daily total of survey results from customers who are reporting that they did not purchase an item due to an empty shelf per store. The data source is from all stores POS survey and downloaded daily at midnight. The total is then divided by the total number of stores.	POS Inventory Items per Store	
Documented standard process	• Defined need • Resources not available	Percentage of formal SOPs in place divided by total SOPs possible. SOP audit of processes outlined by Six Sigma team relative to the process maps built for the Measure phase. Check sheet method used to tally if a formal SOP was published and distributed to those affected.	Existing SOP%	100%
	• Weak training • No training log • No audit	Percentage of the number of positive responses (yes) relative to survey question by total responses. The survey question will be presented to the stakeholder groups, percent responded will be calculated overall and broken down by rating group. "Do you know the store operating procedures that affect you?"	Knowledge of Existing SOP%	100% yes

Figure 5.71 (continued).

Name	Description	Explanation
Jazy Clothing	0% empty shelves	Jazy always prides itself on providing demanded product 100% of the time. No customer leaves the store without their intended purchase. The company must find that the holding cost of the clothing and accessories must be less than the lost business, plus their market research must be strong to forecast demand that well. The clothing is moderately priced, so mark-up is not used as a single method to cover holding cost. Also, the company has been profitable for the last 12 years.
Bmart	Smallest trailer fleet per store	Bmart operates its supply chain efficiently by budgeting for a base demand, while outsourcing for large demand trends. Doing this keeps operating cost low and efficiencies high during medium demand periods. Relative efficiencies remain high due to the contracted trailers and drivers, while operating costs rise marginally due to the outsourcing.
Big Brownie	0% lost equipment	Big Brownie tracks all resources via satellite communications and knows the status, location, and operation of all assets 24/7. Technology has recently allowed this application at a reasonable cost. If power is disconnected from the transponder, the associated database remembers where the equipment last sent a signal.
Yoda	Best practice for lean	Developers and users of lean practices show that Lean works if applied correctly in an embracing environment. Not a benchmark for a metric, but a benchmark for implementation.

Figure 5.72 Benchmarking matrix.

maintenance. First, the check sheet for the trailer audit was simple but effective. They needed to document the incorrect and the correct tallies of a trailer's status, as shown in Figure 5.73. The auditor would look up a random trailer and then contact the location where it was supposed to be. Somebody at that location would confirm if the trailer was really there or not. The auditor then marked the tally of incorrect or correct status reports. This was continued for approximately 52 hours

Defect Type	Tally	Total
Incorrect Status	/////+/////+///	13
Correct Status	/////+/////+/////+/////+///// +/////+/////+/////+///// +/////+/////+/////+///// +/////+/////+/////+///// +/////+/////+/////+///// +/////+////	114
* Day one audit totals		

Figure 5.73   Trailer status check sheets.

from start to stop. Different auditors would take a shift and then hand it off to the next person on duty.

Next, the team started planning the attribute gauge R&R. To document the data necessary for the planned attribute gauge R&R, the team needed to collect data on the dispatch Trailer Log maintenance process. The goal was to know if the driver coordinator consistently updated the log as the process intended. This would help validate the data within the Trailer Log that they were using for the majority of the project's data. If they found that the input was not repeatable and reproducible, then they would need to evaluate the data for errors and/or change the data-collection plan to reflect the use of future planned data-collection events.

A modified check sheet was used to document whether the driver coordinator logged the information at the proper time (or at all) in the process, and if the information was correctly input. If both of these actions were verified as true, then that event of the process was given one point. The scenario types to follow are listed

Dispatch Scenario	Total Events
Warehouse to Store (WS)	7
Store to Depot (SD)	5
Store to Vendor (SV)	7
Depot to Vendor (DV)	7
Vendor to Warehouse (VW)	5

Figure 5.74   Dispatch scenario for gauge R&R study.

- Trends
  - Seasonal trends for both %Utilization and Daily Shipments
  - LOS%, no trend evident from graph
  - AOL%, rates drop at the end of the year
  - Mean dispatch time increases at the end of the year
- Distribution and Outliers
  - Non-normal distribution typical
  - Outliers due to seasonal trend
- Relationship Between
  - Daily shipments and %Trailer Utilization normal
  - Daily shipments and Late AOS or Mean dispatch time show a relationship after 22,000 shipments

Figure 5.75   Database summary.

in Figure 5.74, along with each event total. A summary of the trends is given in Figure 5.75.

Plots, Capability, and Statistics

Paul Jones and Anita were designated as the team's statistical experts. For most people, the best way to understand data is through graphical representation. They decided to use Pareto charts and pie charts for the survey data.

The Trailer Log data was best presented by time-series charts, histograms, and box plots. The team also used a capability study to chart the live-unload times based on a 60 ± 10-minute specification. The majority of the baseline data was generated through the graphical summary chart and the control chart functions in a statistical analysis software package.

Pareto Charts, Time Series, Histograms

Based on the data collected, trend analyses were performed on the metrics, and the distributions were plotted to show outliers, as shown in Figures 5.76–5.90 (Data Figures 5.76–5.90). The data for these analyses came from the Trailer Plan log database and the data collected based on the data-collection plan.

As shown in Figure 5.76, the daily shipments follow a seasonal trend. The team noted that the two points close

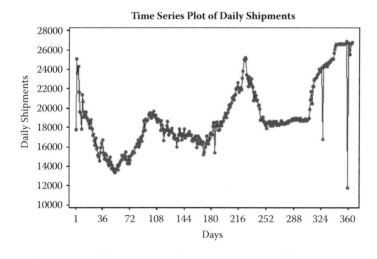

Figure 5.76 Trend analysis of daily shipments.

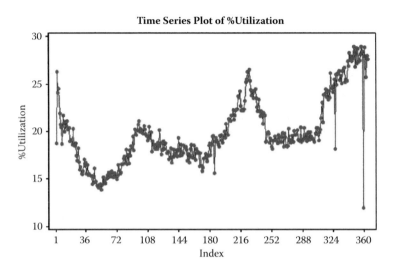

Figure 5.77   Trend analysis of %Utilization.

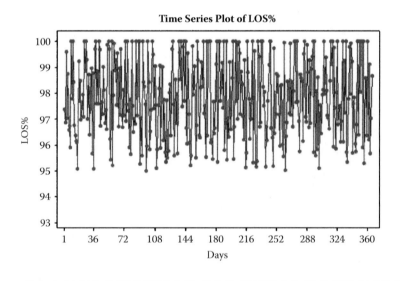

Figure 5.78   Trend analysis of LOS%.

to days 324 and 360 that appeared to be outliers represented Thanksgiving and Christmas holidays, when the depots were on skeleton crews.

The team also noted that the %trailer utilization followed a seasonal pattern, as they expected. This made

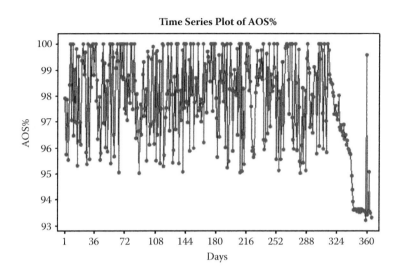

Figure 5.79   Trend analysis of AOS%.

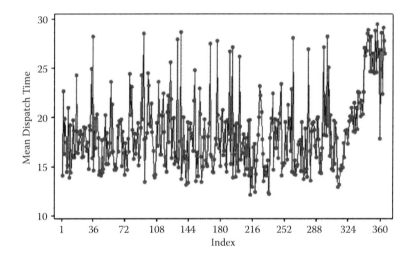

Figure 5.80   Trend analysis of mean dispatch time.

sense to the team based on demand. Jim also commented that he had expected the pattern to be very similar to the daily shipment pattern.

The team was somewhat surprised that the leave-on-schedule (LOS) percentage did not follow a trend. Anita

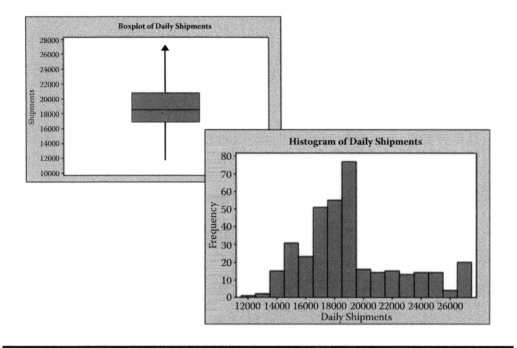

Figure 5.81 Daily shipments data analysis.

had hoped that this time series would provide some interesting insight into a trend based on seasons.

For the arrive-on-schedule (AOS) metric, the team was surprised to find a significant drop at the end of the year. The team thought that this might be due to bad weather that made the trucks run late. However, they could not conclusively identify the cause. Therefore, the team made a special note that further analysis needed to be performed.

The team next examined the time-series trend for mean dispatch time. Again, the team noted a change toward the end of the year. Anita had a hunch that the average dispatch time was taking longer because the volume of shipments was increasing during the holidays. However, the time series did not provide conclusive

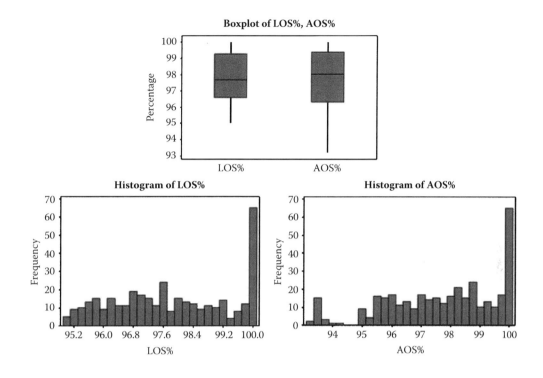

Figure 5.82   AOS% and LOS% data analysis.

evidence of the relationship. Therefore, the team also needed to analyze this metric in further detail.

Using the same data from the Trailer Plan log database, the team created histograms that were used to determine whether the data was normal or centered, and how wide the distributions were. Figures 5.82–5.86 (Data Figures 5.82–5.86) show the histograms and summary statistic for each metric.

Anita noted that the data on daily shipments did not appear to be one distribution, but probably several distributions. The data to the right (above 20,000 daily shipments) seemed to follow more of a uniform distribution. In addition, she commented that the spread of the distribution was very wide, which indicates variation.

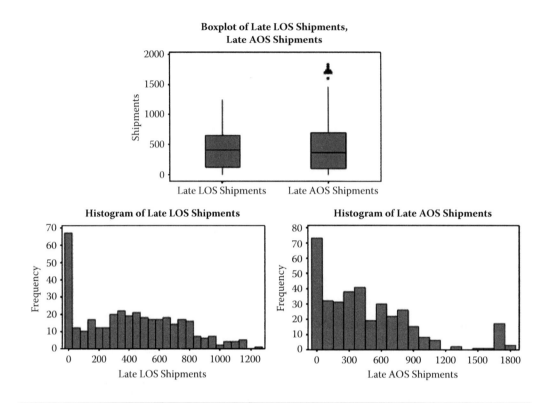

Figure 5.83   Late AOS and late LOS data analysis.

The team felt that a relationship might exist between the leave-on-schedule and arrive-on-schedule metrics. Therefore, the team analyzed the histograms for both metrics together. A clear distribution was not evident, and there was considerable variation. As shown in the box plot at the top of Figure 5.82, more variation exists in the arrive-on-schedule metric.

Based on the information for the leave-on-schedule (LOS) and arrive-on-schedule (AOS) metrics, the team decided to analyze the late shipments to see if there was a trend. The team plotted the frequency of late shipments for those shipments that left on time (but arrived late) and arrived on time (but left late). For the late LOS shipments, two distributions appeared. The highest bar

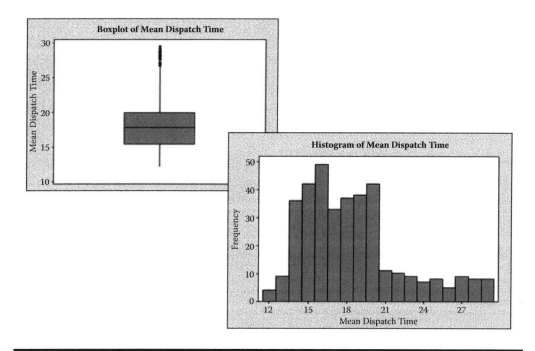

Figure 5.84   Mean dispatch time data analysis.

at zero late LOS shipments represents those that arrived on time; therefore, the frequency is high. There is a wider distribution that appears to center around 500. For late AOS shipments, the team noticed that the distribution skews toward zero.

The team also developed a histogram for the mean dispatch time. Here again, the team found multiple distributions. Data summaries for daily shipments and mean dispatch time were created to provide more statistical information relative to the data. The summaries are provided in Figures 5.85 and 5.86 (Data Figures 5.85 and 5.86).

Next, the team created scatter plots to analyze the relationships between sets of variables. The relevant variables were paired with each other and plotted, as shown in Figures 5.88–5.90 (Data Figures 5.88–5.90).

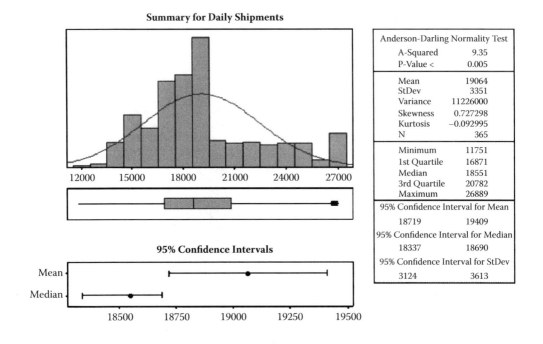

Figure 5.85   Data summary for daily shipments.

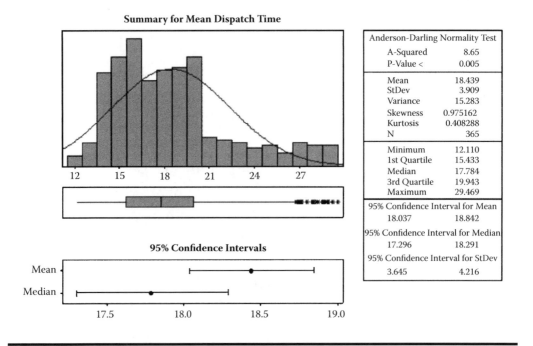

Figure 5.86   Data summary for mean dispatch time.

A clear correlation is shown between %trailer utilization and daily shipments, as shown in Figure 5.87 (Data Figure 5.87). The team expected there would be a strong relationship between these two metrics, because an increase in daily shipments from the distribution center should correspond with an increase in the use of trailers.

Anita found the relationship between daily shipments and leave-on-schedule shipments very interesting (Figure 5.88, Data Figure 5.88). When fewer than 22,000 daily shipments are made, there is not a strong relationship with arriving late. However, when more than 22,000 daily shipments occur, the distribution centers cannot handle the demand, and late shipments increase almost linearly with the number of daily shipments.

The team determined that the relationship between mean dispatch time and daily shipments (Figure 5.89, Data Figure 5.89) was very similar to the relationship between late AOS and daily shipments. Daily shipments

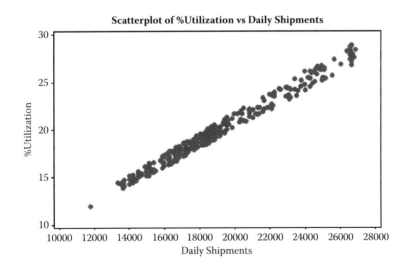

Figure 5.87   Relationship analysis of %utilization and daily shipments.

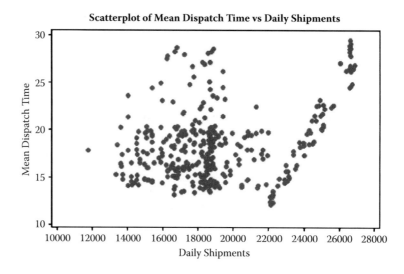

Figure 5.88   Relationship analysis of mean dispatch time and daily shipments.

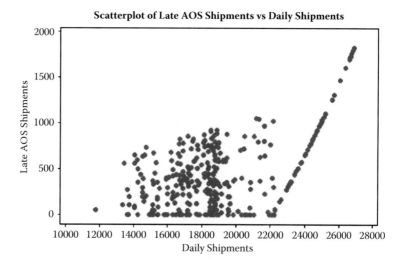

Figure 5.89   Relationship analysis of late AOS and daily shipments.

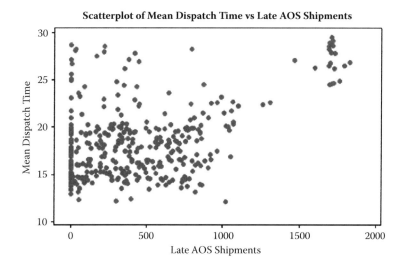

Figure 5.90 Relationship analysis of mean dispatch time and late AOS.

below 22,000 showed no relationship with mean dispatch time. However, here again, the team discovered that when daily shipments are 22,000 or more, the mean dispatch time increases as well.

Finally, the team did not find a relationship between late AOS shipments and mean dispatch time (Figure 5.90, Data Figure 5.90).

Validate Measurement System

The team planned to perform two types of gauge R&Rs within the Measure phase. The first was an attribute study on the performance of the driver coordinator's ability to log information correctly and at the right time. This was previously discussed in the check sheet step. The output from the check sheet was then summarized, as seen in Figures 5.91–5.93 (Data Figures 5.91–5.93).

Sample	Disp. Type	Events	Driver Coord #1		Driver Coord #2		Driver Coord #3	
			Trial 1	Trial 2	Trial 1	Trial 2	Trial 1	Trial 2
1	WS	7	7	6	5	7	7	7
2	SD	5	5	5	5	5	5	5
3	SV	7	7	7	7	7	7	7
4	DV	7	7	7	7	7	7	7
5	VW	5	5	5	5	5	5	5
6	WS	7	7	7	7	7	7	7
7	SD	5	5	5	5	5	5	5
8	SV	7	7	5	7	5	7	6
9	DV	7	7	7	7	6	7	7
10	VW	5	5	5	5	5	5	5

Figure 5.91   Gauge R&R study setup.

Sample	Disp. Type	Events	Driver Coord #1		Driver Coord #2		Driver Coord #3	
			Trial 1	Trial 2	Trial 1	Trial 2	Trial 1	Trial 2
1	WS	7	PASS	FAIL	FAIL	PASS	PASS	PASS
2	SD	5	PASS	PASS	PASS	PASS	PASS	PASS
3	SV	7	PASS	PASS	PASS	PASS	PASS	PASS
4	DV	7	PASS	PASS	PASS	PASS	PASS	PASS
5	VW	5	PASS	PASS	PASS	PASS	PASS	PASS
6	WS	7	PASS	PASS	PASS	PASS	PASS	PASS
7	SD	5	PASS	PASS	PASS	PASS	PASS	PASS
8	SV	7	PASS	FAIL	PASS	FAIL	PASS	FAIL
9	DV	7	PASS	PASS	PASS	FAIL	PASS	PASS
10	VW	5	PASS	PASS	PASS	PASS	PASS	PASS

Figure 5.92   Gauge R&R data collection.

Attribute Gauge R& R Effectiveness

SCORING REPORT	
DATE:	3/10/2008
NAME:	Mike O'Conner
PRODUCT:	Dispatch Process
BUSINESS:	Transportation

Attribute Legend
1 pass
2 fail

Known Population		Operator #1		Operator #2		Operator #3		Y/N Agree	Y/N Agree
Sample	Attribute	Try #1	Try #2	Try #1	Try #2	Try #1	Try #2		
1	pass	pass	fail	fail	pass	pass	pass	N	N
2	pass	pass	pass	pass	pass	pass	pass	Y	Y
3	pass	pass	pass	pass	pass	pass	pass	Y	Y
4	pass	pass	pass	pass	pass	pass	pass	Y	Y
5	pass	pass	pass	pass	pass	pass	pass	Y	Y
6	pass	pass	pass	pass	pass	pass	pass	Y	Y
7	pass	pass	pass	pass	pass	pass	pass	Y	Y
8	pass	pass	fail	pass	fail	pass	fail	N	N
9	pass	pass	pass	pass	fail	pass	pass	N	N
10	pass	pass	pass	pass	pass	pass	pass	Y	Y
% APPRAISER SCORE(1)->		80.00%		70.00%		90.00%			
% SCORE VS. ATTRIBUTE(2)->		80.00%		70.00%		90.00%			

	SCREEN % EFFECTIVE SCORE(3)->	70.00%
	SCREEN % EFFECTIVE SCORE vs. ATTRIBUTE(4)->	70.00%

Figure 5.93

The next gauge R&R was a variable study on the live unload time. This was to be performed at three different stores, with 10 different trucks (all similar loads), and repeated three times. The team noted that this type of study is typically done to look for the variation in the measurement tool. But a gauge R&R examines a measurement system that consists of parts (trucks), operators (stores), and the measurement device itself, a stopwatch. The specification to be used was 60 ± 10 minutes, so the variation due to the measurement device was not an issue. The variation that was present was within the store and the trucks. The team assumed that the trucks would be very similarly packed, and that the main variation would be seen in the store/operators. The data used for the study appears in Figures 5.94–5.96 (Data Figures 5.94–5.96).

Truck	Std Time	Store A			Store B			Store C		
+/- 10 min		Trial 1	Trial 2	Trial 3	Trial 1	Trial 2	Trial 3	Trial 1	Trial 2	Trial 3
1	60	71	73	77	61	62	48	65	78	56
2	60	64	77	63	52	58	55	66	56	77
3	60	72	72	68	56	45	48	56	53	75
4	60	61	61	76	64	49	50	54	78	77
5	60	59	62	75	58	55	54	81	58	78
6	60	12	71	64	46	57	46	81	84	82
7	60	65	73	65	55	54	48	57	70	62
8	60	57	60	69	62	45	48	80	82	61
9	60	70	69	69	54	51	48	85	62	73
10	60	62	75	59	54	47	47	76	61	76

Figure 5.94   Gauge R&R data collection.

Gauge R&R Study for Unload Time-XBar/R Method

Source	VarComp	% Contribution (% of VarComp)
Total Gauge R&R	138.854	97.13
Repeatability	57.460	40.19
Reproducibility	81.394	56.93
Part-To-Part	4.107	2.87
Total Variation	142.961	100.00

Process Tolerance = 20

Source	Study Var StdDev (SD)	% Study Var (6 * SD)	% Tolerance (%SV)	(SV/Toler)
Total Gauge R&R	11.7836	70.7018	98.55	353.51
Repeatability	7.5802	45.4814	63.40	227.41
Reproducibility	9.0219	54.1312	75.45	270.66
Part-To-Part	2.0266	12.1593	16.95	60.80
Total Variation	11.9566	71.7398	100.00	358.70

Number of Distinct Categories = 1

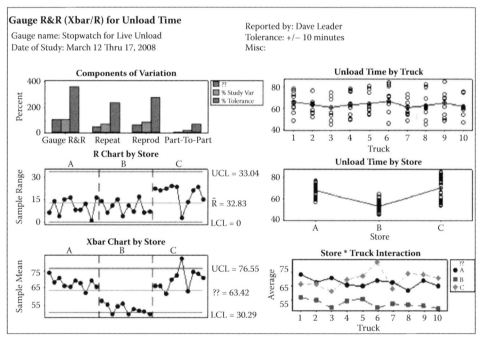

Figure 5.95   Gauge R&R report for live unload study.

Define the Cost of Poor Quality (COPQ) and Cost/Benefit

Based on the process maps, metrics, and knowledge of the trailer utilization process, the team brainstormed the possible costs of poor quality. All costs were considered, including preventive, appraisal, failure, and intangible costs. A list of potential costs for each respective area is given in Figure 5.96.

Moving to the Analyze Phase

As the team prepared to move forward to the next phase, the team members held a meeting to determine the next steps. The team identified the following steps:

1. Complete a comprehensive statistical analysis of all the data collected from surveys and the Trailer Log database.
2. Develop cause-and-effect relationships.
3. Determine and validate brainstormed root causes.
4. Collect more data if needed to validate root causes.
5. Identify short- and long-term improvements based on the statistical data collected.
6. Complete cost/benefit analysis.
7. Prepare the Analyze report and presentation.

Prevention Costs	Appraisal Costs	External Costs	Internal Costs	Intangible Costs
1. Creation of SOPs and training of the material 2. Weekly team meetings with Driver Coordinators to review current performance 3. Trailer quantity held to meet highest level of demand 4. Driver quantity held to meet highest level of demand 5. Trailer maintenance	1. Trailer Log Database query for the AOS% and LOS% 2. Time and materials associated with driver's communication of leave time and arrival time to Driver Coordinator 3. Time and materials associated with Driver Coordinator's creation, logging, and communication of ETL and ETA to driver	1. Missed sale due to zero shelf inventory 2. Lost customer due to lack of faith that what they want will be on the shelf	1. Late shipments cause potential down time or create the need to redirect personnel until the shipment arrives 2. Late shipments may increase risk of personnel injury due to a need to catch up while unloading or stocking the late items	1. Damaged corporate image, "best price, if it is on the shelf"? 2. Internal corporate conflict may build resistance to future cooperation

Figure 5.96

Chapter 6

Analyze Phase

Introduction

Now that the team had established a baseline of the process and gained the voice of the customer, they needed to do some problem solving. In the Analyze phase, the team needs to focus on identifying potential root causes of the problem: improve trailer utilization. They also need to validate cause-and-effect relationships between the key process input variables and the key process output variables. By doing this, the team should be able to identify the vital few root causes of the problem. As expected, the team was given a set of questions by their team leader, Anita, for the first meeting of the Analyze phase.

- What is the current state?
- What are the root causes that impact the process?
- Can we validate the root causes identified?
- Is the current state as good as the process can do?
- How does the root process perform? (variation and target)

- What inputs should be changed to improve the root cause?
- Do we have adequate data on the root cause of the process?
- Who will help make changes?
- What resources will we need?
- What could cause this change effort to fail?
- What major obstacles do we face in completing this project?

Many members wanted to jump to the solution and fix the problem now, but Anita wouldn't let them. Anita and Jim together explained that this process was structured and had a reason for each phase. The data would give them the answer. So, each member agreed to work as planned. During the meeting, Anita explained the activities and deliverables (Figure 6.1), and each member volunteered for a share of the work.

Analyze Activities		*Deliverables*
1	Develop Cause-and-Effect Relationships	1) Cause & Effect Diagram and Why–Why
		2) Test for Normality
		3) Process Analysis and 8 Wastes
		4) 5S
		5) Failure Mode and Effects Analysis
2	Determine Valid Root Causes	6) Correlation Analysis
		7) Regression Analysis
		8) Hypothesis Tests
3	Develop Process Capability	9) Control Charts
		10) Capability

Figure 6.1   Analyze phase activities and deliverables.

Develop Cause-and-Effect Relationships

Kicking off the Analyze phase, Anita scheduled a team meeting to begin finding the root cause of low trailer utilization (%trailer utilization). Brainstorming was the first method to bring forth information, and that information was channeled into a few cause-and-effect diagrams. Jim Pulls also suggested using why–why diagrams. He liked using both, even on the same topic. He explained that the cause-and-effect diagram forces a team to think in specific domains, but the why–why is open to all possibilities. So the team agreed to do both for %trailer utilization. They started with the cause-and-effect diagram, for which they tried using the original categories: Measurement, Method, Machine, People, Materials, and Environment. These categories did not fit very well, so, referring to their System Model Map, shown again in Figure 6.2, they replaced the original categories with the main inputs of the map.

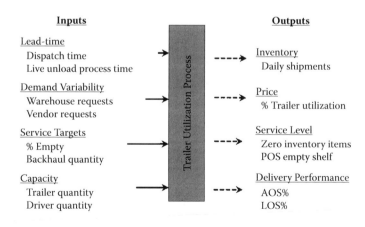

Figure 6.2   System Model map for utilization process.

% Trailer Utilization Low		
Lead Time	*Demand*	*Resource Capacity*
• Mean dispatch time high • Live unload count or time too high	• Seasonal demand *Service Targets* • %Empty	• Fixed driver count too low • Fixed trailer count too high • Fixed coordinator count too low • Drop and Hook count too high • Misplaced trailers • Idle trailers

Figure 6.3   Cause-and-effect brainstorming ideas.

By doing this, they assumed that %trailer utilization was affected by lead time, demand variability, service targets, and capacity. Any causes within the process will be brought out with the why–why diagram. Figure 6.3 shows the beginning of the brainstorm session's ideas. The effect they were working on was low %trailer utilization. More ideas were added, and a full cause-and-effect diagram was built, as shown in Figure 6.4. Some subcategories were then analyzed with the why–why method. Also, Jim did not let his team get away without doing a why–why on low %trailer utilization, as shown in Figure 6.5. They found that the why–why tool exposed a few new topics of discussion. One topic, for example, was idle trailers, as shown in Figure 6.6.

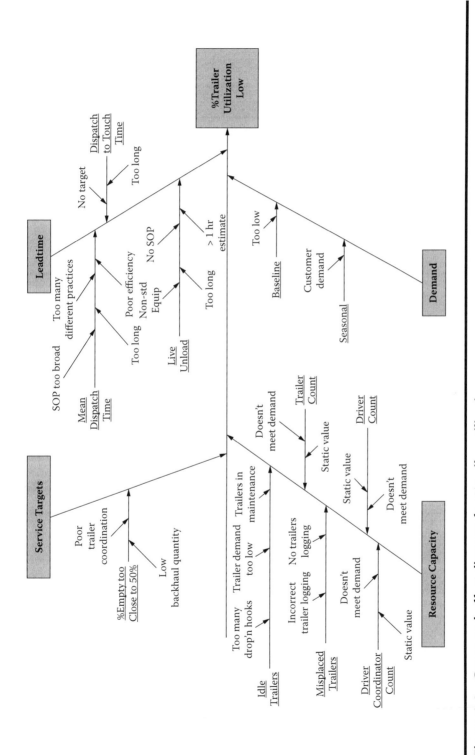

Figure 6.4 Cause-and-effect diagram for %trailer utilization.

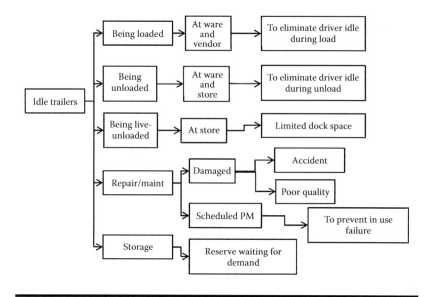

Figure 6.5   Why–why diagram on idle trailers.

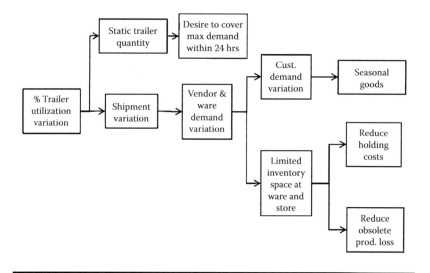

Figure 6.6   Why–why diagram on %trailer utilization variation.

Test for Normality Exercise

As seen from the baseline in the Measure phase, none of the metrics have data that was considered to be normal. Due to the seasonality of the customer demand, the team found that the data had three or four separate

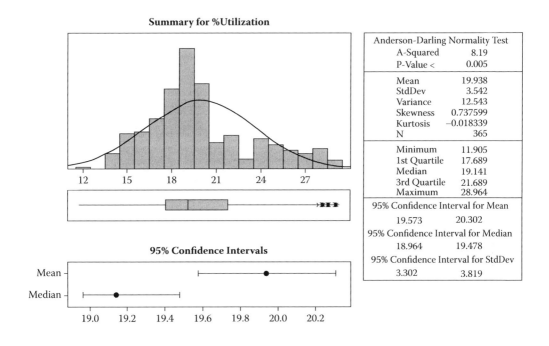

Figure 6.7   Test for normality.

distributions, depending on how one would define a season, as shown in Figure 6.7 (Data Figure 6.7). Normality tests were performed for each metric and are summarized in Figure 6.8 (Data Figure 6.8).

Process Analysis and 8 Wastes

While looking for root causes, the team understood that it was also a good time to examine the process for wastes. This marks the beginning of the team's effort to combine Lean and Six Sigma. The 8-wastes method was used when examining all of the processes identified in the Measure phase. At this time, the team agreed not to examine processes beyond those identified, but to keep a record of possible candidates that might emerge

Metric	Baseline
%Trailer Utilization	Mean = 19.938%; StdDev = 3.543; Max = 28.964; Min = 11.905; UCL = 22.26; LCL = 17.61. **Distribution is not normal**. Trend is seasonal and follows Daily Shipments.
Daily Shipments	Mean = 19,064; StdDev = 3,351; Max = 26,889; Min = 11,751; UCL = 20,468; LCL = 17,660. **Distribution is not normal**. Trend is seasonal.
%Empty	Mean = 47.41%; StdDev = 1.438%; Max = 49.977%; Min = 43.314%; UCL = 50.617%; LCL = 47.094%. **Distribution is not normal**. Trend shows special cause in the last few weeks of the year.
AOS%	Mean = 97.73%; StdDev = 1.851%; Max = 100%; Min = 93.202%; UCL = 102.088%; LCL = 93.373%. **Distribution is not normal**.
LOS%	Mean = 97.833%; StdDev = 1.563%; Max = 100%; Min = 95.005%; UCL = 102.83%; LCL = 92.83%. **Distribution is not normal**.
Dispatch Mean	Mean = 18.439; StdDev = 3.909; Max = 29.469; Min = 12.110; UCL = 27.34; LCL = 9.54. **Distribution is not normal**.
Dispatch Deviation Mean	Mean = −11.561; StdDev = 3.909; Max = −0.531; Min = −17.89; UCL = −2.66; LCL = −20.46. **Distribution is not normal**.
Arrival Deviation Mean	Mean = −28.993; StdDev = 12.502; Max = 7.047; Min = −45.484; UCL = −11.20; LCL = −46.79. **Distribution is not normal**.
Departure Deviation Mean	Mean = −34.638; StdDev = 11.441; Max = −6.497; Min = −55.329; UCL = −11.03; LCL = −58.24. **Distribution is not normal**.
Live Unload Process Time	Mean = 63.422; StdDev = 10.876; Max = 85.0; Min = 45.0; UCL = 102.67; LCL = 24.18. **Distribution is not normal**.

Figure 6.8   Summary of normality tests.

Metric	Baseline
Zero-inventory items per store	Mean = 16.372; StdDev = 11.558; Max = 49.4; Min = 8.7; UCL = 22.49; LCL = 10.26. **Distribution is not normal**.
POS Empty Shelf survey per store (2 weeks)	Mean = 2.5214; StdDev = 0.6841; Max = 4.0; Min = 1.9; UCL = 4.383; LCL = 0.66. **Distribution is not normal**.

Figure 6.8 (continued).

during the project work. The eight categories used to identify waste and some examples are listed as follows:

- Transportation: moving people, products, or information
- Overproduction: making more than is immediately required
- Motion: bending, turning, reaching, or lifting
- Defects: rework, scrap, or incorrect documentation
- Delay: waiting for parts, information, instructions, or equipment
- Inventory: storing parts, pieces, or documentation ahead of requirements
- Processing: tolerances too tight or specifications beyond need
- People skills: underutilizing capabilities, delegating tasks with inadequate training

Using these categories of waste, the process was analyzed and wastes were identified, as shown in Figure 6.9.

Waste	Process	Process Step	Details Plus Suggestion
Delay	Trailer Request —Warehouse	Request empty trailer at specified dock	Remove the wait for an empty trailer at Warehouse. All empty loading docks should have a request for empty sent as soon as a full trailer leaves the dock.
Delay	Trailer Request —Vendor	Request empty trailer at specified dock	Driver Coordinator to send an empty when a Vendor requests a pickup. This will prevent waiting for an empty.
Delay	Trailer Request —Depot	Request trailer to be delivered to Depot, empty	Depot to only PM those trailers in lot. If not in lot, then the trailer will be quarantined when it does come in.
People Skills	Dispatch Plan Maintenance	B1 thru END	Establish a team of D–W–D drivers that work directly for Warehouse and Depot. This will reduce workload for Driver Coordinator and streamline communication.
Delay	Dispatch Plan Maintenance	Wait for Driver to call in (C1 leg)	Mitigate delay by assigning a Driver Coord. to watch level of drivers available and contact contractors when necessary.

Figure 6.9   Process analysis and eight wastes.

5S

With the understanding that 5S is an on-site tool, the team broke into groups to examine the driver coordinator's work environment and the store's live-unloading process area. The goal was to establish a baseline and use this same exercise to establish control within these

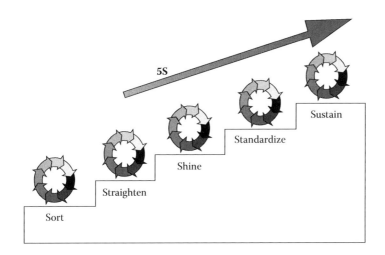

Figure 6.10   5S card.

two areas that were deemed critical to the trailer utilization process. While doing their analysis, the team referenced a card that was given to each member by Jim Pulls. The 5Ss are Japanese and don't directly translate into five English S words, but this card had five English S words that matched very closely. Figure 6.10 is a copy of the card. Figure 6.11 provides the 5S evaluation sheet used. Figures 6.12 and 6.13 show the 5S sheets for the office and dock, respectively.

Failure Mode and Effects Analysis

Mike O'Conner was in charge of the next tool, Failure Mode and Effects Analysis (FMEA). He had seen its power when used for a manufacturing process and knew that it would benefit the team when used for the trailer utilization process. The team used high-level processes that were identified as causes to the effects examined via the

5S Evaluation Sheet	
Office	*Store Dock*
1S Sort (Seiri)—Organize needed from unneeded, remove the unneeded.	
Are only necessary materials or documents present?	Are only necessary materials or equipment present?
Are problem documents or issues identified and segregated?	Are defective materials or equipment identified and segregated?
Are unused machines, equipment, or resources marked with a red tag?	Are unused machines, equipment, or materials marked with a red tag?
Are red tagged items in the red tag area?	Are red tagged items in the red tag area?
Is standard work present and current?	Is standard work present and current?
2S Straighten (Seiton)—Arrange neatly, identify for ease of use.	
Are areas and walkways clearly marked?	Are areas and walkways clearly marked?
Are materials visually controlled with location indicators and at the point of use?	Are materials visually controlled with location indicators and at the point of use?
Are maximum and minimum allowable quantities indicated?	Are maximum and minimum allowable quantities indicated?
Is nonconforming material segregated, identified, and documented?	Is nonconforming material segregated, identified, and documented?
Are equipment and tools clearly identified and arranged in order of use?	Are equipment and tools clearly identified and arranged in order of use?
3S Shine (Seiso)—Conduct a cleanup campaign to polish and shine the area.	
Are floors and areas clean and free of trash, liquids, and dirt?	Are floors and areas clean and free of trash, liquids, and dirt?
Is equipment inspection combined with equipment maintenance?	Is equipment inspection combined with equipment maintenance?
Is the work area sufficiently lit, ventilated, and free of dust and odors?	Is the work area sufficiently lit, ventilated, and free of dust and odors?

Figure 6.11   5S evaluation sheet.

5S Evaluation Sheet	
Office	*Store Dock*
Are cleaning operations assigned and visually managed?	Are cleaning operations assigned and visually managed?
Are cleaning supplies easily available and stored in a marked area?	Are cleaning supplies easily available and stored in a marked area?
4S Standardize (Seiketsu)—Continue the habits frequently and often.	
Are standard procedures clear, documented, and actively used?	Are standard procedures clear, documented, and actively used?
Do the records of problem documents or issues have a corrective action?	Do the records of defective materials have a corrective action?
Are equipment Preventive Maintenance (PM) procedures in place and current?	Are equipment Preventative Maintenance (PM) procedures in place and current?
Are waste and recyclable material receptacles emptied regularly?	Are waste and recyclable material receptacles emptied regularly?
Are scrap and product nonconformance areas cleared at a set interval?	Are scrap and product nonconformance areas cleared at a set interval?
5S Sustain (Shitsuke)—Institute the 5 S practices as a part of the culture.	
The 5th S is awarded when 3 consecutive months of 1S, 2S, 3S, and 4S have been sustained.	The 5th S is awarded when 3 consecutive months of 1S, 2S, 3S, and 4S have been sustained.

Figure 6.11 (continued).

cause-and-effect diagrams. For example, the live-unload and the dispatch processes were identified to cause low %trailer utilization values. These two processes were then evaluated by completing the FMEA form that Jim Pulls had supplied, as shown in Figure 6.14.

	Mar		Apr	
Office	Y	N	Y	N
1S Sort (Seiri)—Organize needed from unneeded, remove the unneeded.				
Are only necessary materials or documents present?				
Are problem documents or issues identified and segregated?				
Are unused machines, equipment, or resources marked with a red tag?				
Are red tagged items in the red tag area?				
Is standard work present and current?				
2S Straighten (Seiton)—Arrange neatly, identify for ease of use.				
Are areas and walkways clearly marked?				
Are materials visually controlled with location indicators and at the point of use?				
Are maximum and minimum allowable quantities indicated?				
Is nonconforming material segregated, identified, and documented?				
Are equipment and tools clearly identified and arranged in order of use?				
3S Shine (Seiso)—Conduct a cleanup campaign to polish and shine the area.				
Are floors and areas clean and free of trash, liquids, and dirt?				
Is equipment inspection combined with equipment maintenance?				
Is the work area sufficiently lit, ventilated, and free of dust and odors?				
Are cleaning operations assigned and visually managed?				
Are cleaning supplies easily available and stored in a marked area?				

Figure 6.12   5S evaluation sheet for office.

		Mar		Apr	
Office		*Y*	*N*	*Y*	*N*
4S Standardize (Seiketsu)—Continue the habits frequently and often.					
Are standard procedures clear, documented, and actively used?					
Do the records of problem documents or issues have a corrective action?					
Are equipment Preventive Maintenance (PM) procedures in place and current?					
Are waste and recyclable material receptacles emptied regularly?					
Are scrap and product nonconformance areas cleared at a set interval?					
5S Sustain (Shitsuke)—Institute the 5 S practices as a part of the culture					
The 5th S is awarded when 3 consecutive months of 1S, 2S, 3S, and 4S have been sustained.					

Figure 6.12   (continued).

Determine and Validate Root Causes

From the cause-and-effect and why–why diagrams, the team understood that %trailer utilization was connected with quite a few of the metrics for which they had gathered data. The next step was to examine how they were related, if at all. The team used correlation analysis to confirm what they understood and what they may have seen in graphs. The following is a list of the null hypotheses which they tried to confirm.

■ Daily shipments correlated to %trailer utilization (Figure 6.15, Data Figure 6.15)

■ Daily shipments correlated to AOS% (Figure 6.16, Data Figure 6.16)

■ %Trailer utilization correlated to AOS% (Figure 6.17, Data Figure 6.17)

■ Zero inventory items correlated to %trailer utilization (Figure 6.18, Data Figure 6.18)

■ Mean dispatch time correlated to %trailer utilization (Figure 6.19, Data Figure 6.19)

■ %Empty correlated to %trailer utilization (Figure 6.20, Data Figure 6.20)

■ Warehouse requests correlated to %trailer utilization (Figure 6.21, Data Figure 6.21)

■ Vendor requests correlated to %trailer utilization (Figure 6.22, Data Figure 6.22)

	Mar		Apr	
Store Dock	*Y*	*N*	*Y*	*N*
1S Sort (Seiri)—Organize needed from unneeded, remove the unneeded.				
Are only necessary materials or equipment present?				
Are defective materials or equipment identified and segregated?				
Are unused machines. equipment, or materials marked with a red tag?				
Are red tagged items in the red tag area?				
Is standard work present and current?				

Figure 6.13   5S sheets for the dock.

		Mar		Apr	
Store Dock		*Y*	*N*	*Y*	*N*
2S Straighten (Seiton)—Arrange neatly, identify for ease of use.					
Are areas and walkways clearly marked?					
Are materials visually controlled with location indicators and at the point of use?					
Are maximum and minimum allowable quantities indicated?					
Is nonconforming material segregated, identified, and documented?					
Are equipment and tools clearly identified and arranged in order of use?					
3S Shine (Seiso)—Conduct a cleanup campaign to polish and shine the area.					
Are floors and areas clean and free of trash, liquids, and dirt?					
Is equipment inspection combined with equipment maintenance?					
Is the work area sufficiently lit, ventilated, and free of dust and odors?					
Are cleaning operations assigned and visually managed?					
Are cleaning supplies easily available and stored in a marked area?					
4S Standardize (Seiketsu)—Continue the habits frequently and often.					
Are standard procedures clear, documented, and actively used?					
Do the records of defective materials have a corrective action?					
Are equipment Preventative Maintenance (PM) procedures in place and current?					
Are waste and recyclable material receptacles emptied regularly?					
Are scrap and product nonconformance areas cleared at a set interval?					
5S Sustain (Shitsuke)—Institute the 5 S practices as a part of the culture.					
The 5th S is awarded when 3 consecutive rnonths of 1S, 2S, 3S, and 4S have been sustained.					

Figure 6.13   (continued).

Process / Product
Failure Modes and Effects Analysis
(FMEA)

Process or Product Name:	Trailer Utilization Process	Prepared by:		Page ____ of ____
Responsible:		FMEA Date (Orig) _____	(Rev) _____	

Process Function	Potential Failure Mode	Potential Effects of Failure	S E V	Potential Cause(s)/ Mechanism(s) of Failure	O C C	Current Process Controls	D E T	R P N	Recommended Action(s)	Responsibility and Completion Date
			How severe is the effect to the customer?		How often does the cause of failure mode occur?		How well can you detect cause of failure mode?	SEV x OCC x DET		
The highest value process steps from the C&E matrix.	In what ways does the process potentially fail to meet the process requirements and/or design intent?	What is the effect of each failure mode on the outputs and/or customer requirements? The customer could be the next operations, subsequent operations, another division, or the end user.		How can the failure occur? Describe in terms of something that can be corrected or controlled. Be specific. Try to identify the causes that directly impact the failure mode. i.e., root causes.		What are the existing controls and procedures (inspection and test) that either prevent failure mode from occuring or detect the failure should it occur? **Should include an SOP number.**			What are the actions for reducing the occurrence, or improving detection, or for identifying the root cause if it is unknown? **Should have actions only on high RPNs or easy fixes.**	Who is responsible for the recommended action? What is the due date for completion?

Live Unload Process	Lasts too long	Miss scheduled departure time	3	No best practice used; improper equipment used; no room to put unloaded product	10	none	10	300	Define a best practice that includes equipment list with specifications	Store and Lean Six Sigma Team
Dispatch Process	Incorrect logging of request information	Delayed pickup or delivery of trailer	6	Incorrect request input; illegible request input; typo	4	none	10	240	Define a best practice that instructs how to make a request and control input with a standard form; implement a confirmation process	Transportation and Lean Six Sigma Team

Figure 6.14 Failure modes and effects analysis.

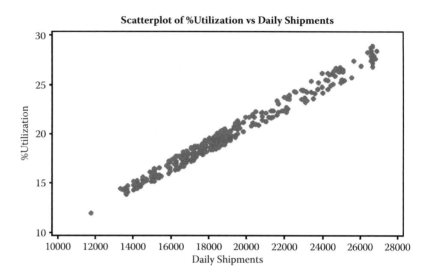

Figure 6.15   Correlation analysis of daily shipments and %trailer utilization.

The team noted a clear relationship between daily shipments and %trailer utilization, as they expected (Figure 6.15, Data Figure 6.15). As the number of daily shipments increased, the number of trailers used also increased. Therefore, the team was able to validate what they expected.

The team also performed a correlation analysis on the relationship between daily shipments and AOS%, as shown in Figure 6.16 (Data Figure 6.16). This analysis provided a similar relationship, as noted in the trend analysis in the Measure phase (Chapter 5, Figures 5.75–5.79). The team noted a lack of a relationship until the number of daily shipments reached 22,000. The team utilized the data for the daily shipments above 22,000 to further investigate the relationship. The bottom left of Figure 6.16 shows a clear and strong relationship. As the number of daily shipments increases, the AOS% decreases in a strong linear pattern.

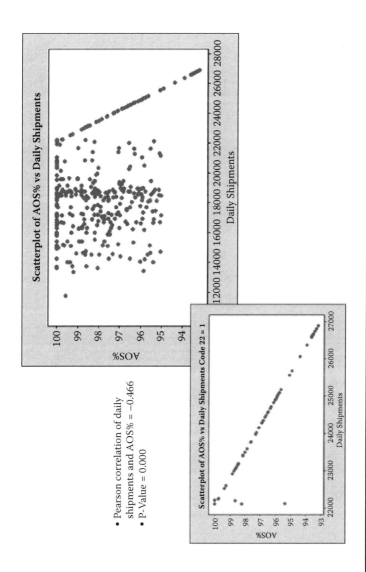

Figure 6.16   Correlation analysis of daily shipments and AOS%.

The team next looked at the relationship between %trailer utilization and AOS% (Figure 6.17, Data Figure 6.17). Using all of the data, no clear trend seemed to appear. Jim, however, thought that a pattern was occurring after the %trailer utilization reached approximately 22%. The team then decided to use the data for %trailer utilization above 22% to see if a trend became evident. As shown in the bottom left corner of Figure 6.17, a moderate relationship appeared. As %trailer utilization increases, the AOS% decreases. The team discussed this relationship and agreed that it did make sense, because the depots struggled to meet the increased demand based on their resource capacity.

The next relationship the team evaluated was between zero inventory items per store and %trailer utilization, as shown in Figure 6.18 (Data Figure 6.18). The team thought that this was an important relationship because they wanted to ensure that the stores had ample stock, as noted in the benchmarking analysis. At first glance, the team did not see a clear overall trend because of the two distinct patterns. Again, Jim wanted to hone in on an area of the graph. In this case, he thought a pattern would emerge when the %trailer utilization was above 22%, similar to the relationship with AOS%. As shown in the bottom left of Figure 6.18, a relationship does emerge. It was stronger than the previous relationship, but was still considered a moderate relationship by the team.

In addition, the team performed a correlation analysis on mean dispatch time and %trailer utilization, as shown in Figure 6.19 (Data Figure 6.19). After discussing how to hone in on subtle trends in the overall data, Simone noticed another trend in this data set when the %trailer

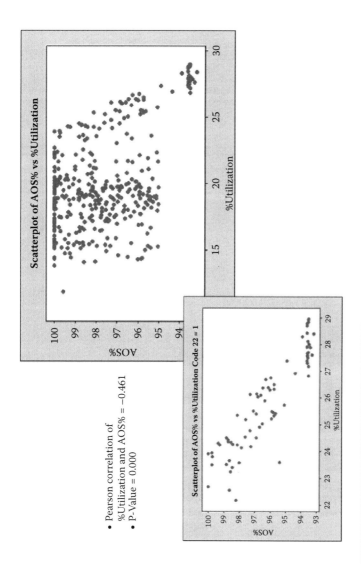

Figure 6.17 Correlation analysis of %trailer utilization and AOS%.

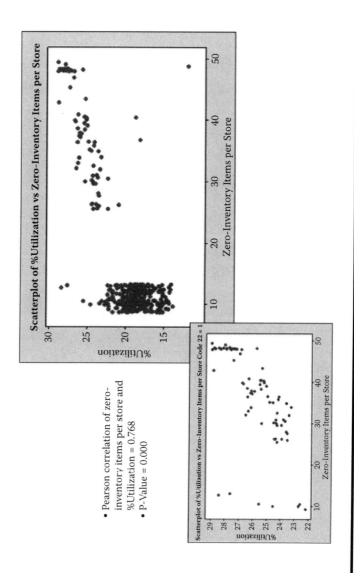

- Pearson correlation of zero-inventory items per store and %Utilization = 0.768
- P-Value = 0.000

Figure 6.18 Correlation analysis of zero inventory items and %trailer utilization.

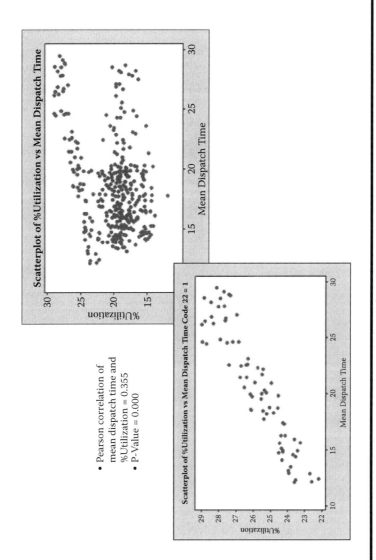

Figure 6.19 **Correlation analysis of mean dispatch time and %trailer utilization.**

utilization was over 22%. The team used this data to perform another correlation analysis, as shown in the bottom left of Figure 6.19. The relationship is moderate but exists here as well.

Next, the team performed a correlation analysis to determine the relationship between %empty and %utilization (Figure 6.20, Data Figure 6.20). The team felt strongly that there would be a distinct relationship between these two factors. After plotting the data, the team was surprised that there was not a strong relationship. Because the previous correlation analyses indicated trends when the %trailer utilization was above 22%, the team decided to hone in on this data as well to see if a stronger trend would appear. As shown in the bottom left of Figure 6.20, a pattern did emerge; however, it was a weak relationship.

Based on the previous analysis and cause-and-effect diagrams, the team also felt that a relationship would exist between the number of warehouse requests and the %trailer utilization. As shown in Figure 6.21 (Data Figure 6.21), a strong relationship did exist. Even though a strong relationship emerged with all the data, the team decided to also hone in on the data for %trailer utilization over 22% to see the trend. Again, a trend emerged here, as expected.

The final correlation analysis the team performed was between the number of vendor requests and %trailer utilization, as shown in Figure 6.22 (Data Figure 6.22). The overall data showed no relationship, so the team again decided to narrow the data down to include only the %trailer utilization over 22%. In this case, however, a pattern did not emerge.

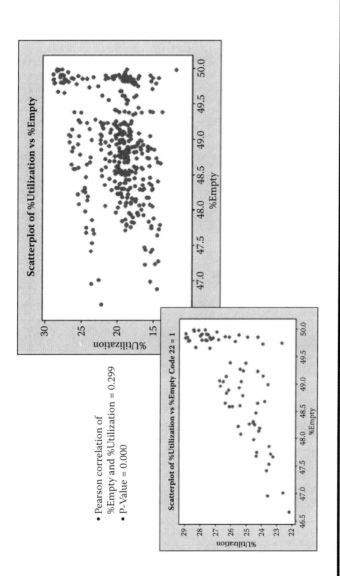

Figure 6.20 Correlation analysis of %empty and %trailer utilization.

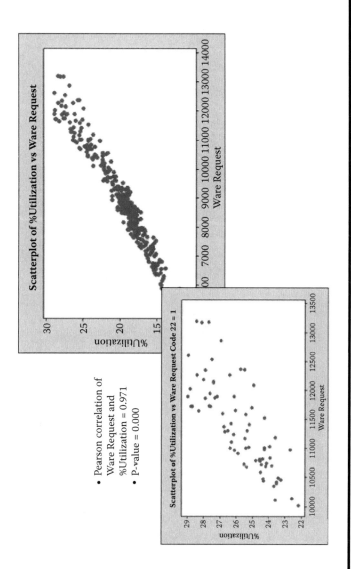

Figure 6.21   Correlation analysis of warehouse requests and %trailer utilization.

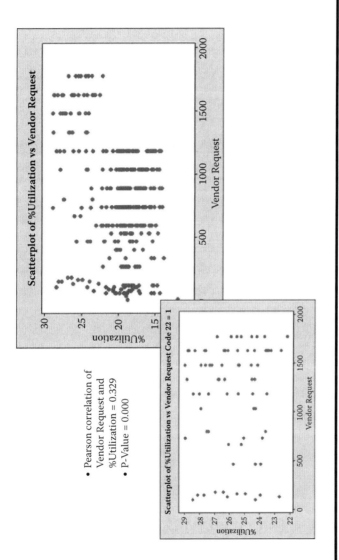

Figure 6.22 Correlation analysis of vendor requests and %trailer utilization.

Regression Analysis

Based upon the results of the correlation analysis, the team wanted to see if they could create a model that would predict %trailer utilization based on inputs to the system. The key contributors were found to be zero inventory items per store (customer demand), warehouse request, and mean dispatch time. The results of the regression analysis are given in Figures 6.23 and 6.24 (Data Figures 6.23 and 6.24).

Hypothesis Test

While plotting the data in scatter plots, the team discovered an interesting trend above 22,000 shipments. Jim Pulls noted that this trend is a special case that must be confirmed. So, the team used hypothesis testing to confirm that the data associated with shipment levels above 22,000 were indeed significantly different compared to the shipments below 22,000. The team wanted to know if the customer is impacted by this special case relative to AOS% and zero inventory items per store. Also, was the mean dispatch time impacted by this shift? The results of these hypothesis tests are given in Figures 6.25–6.27 (Data Figures 6.25–6.27).

Develop Process Capability

To better understand the variation of the process, the team planned to construct control charts. Anita helped the team to understand that they needed to examine all

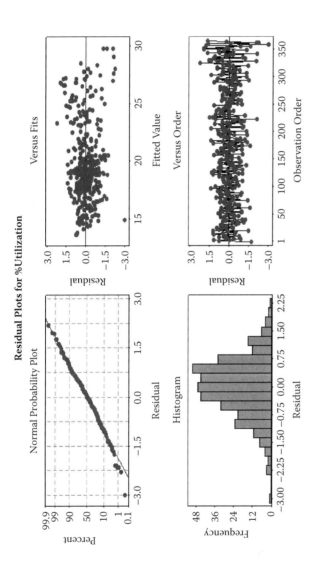

Figure 6.23 Regression analysis for %trailer utilization.

The regression equation is

%Utilization = 1.00 + (0.0367 × Zero-inventory items per store) + (0.00200 × Ware Request) + (0.0211 × Mean Dispatch time)

Predictor	Coeff	SE Coeff	T	P
Constant	0.9997	0.3389	2.95	0.003
Zero-inventory items per store	0.036689	0.005371	6.83	0.000
Ware Request	0.00200353	0.00003939	50.86	0.000
Mean Dispatch time	0.02111	0.01148	1.84	0.067

S = 0.791575	R-Sq = 95.0%	R-Sq(adj) = 95.0%
Analysis of Variance		

Source	DF	SS	MS	F	P
Regression	3	4339.5	1446.5	2308.54	0.000
Residual Error	361	226.2	0.6		
Total	364	4565.7			

Source	DF	Seq SS
Zero-inventory items per store	1	2693.5
Ware Request	1	1643.9
Mean Dispatch time	1	2.1

Figure 6.24 **Regression analysis for %trailer utilization.**

metrics within the project's scope, not just those that directly impacted %trailer utilization. They used the VOP (voice of the process) matrix as a reference to choose which metrics to chart. Because the data was already averaged for the day, it was impossible to take multiple samples per day. Instead, the team built a special variation of the control charts called an IMR (individuals

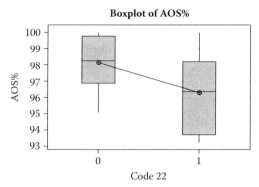

Figure 6.25   AOS% analysis

with moving range) chart, as shown in Figures 6.28–6.33 (Data Figures 6.28–6.33).

Process Capability

The majority of the data was not normal due to the seasonal impact of the customer demand. So, the team agreed to plot the capability of the live-unload data, since they planned to suggest a target and tolerance as part of their recommendations, as shown in Figure 6.34 (Data Figure 6.34). The live-unload data taken for the gauge R&R (repeatability and reproducibility) was charted for capability in reference to the agreed-upon target of 60 minutes and tolerance of plus or minus

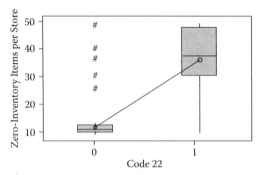

Two-Sample T-Test and CI: Zero-inventory items per store, Code 22

Two-sample Test for Zero-inventory items per store

Code
22	N	Mean	StdDev	SE Mean
0	292	11.45	3.92	0.23
1	73	36.1	11.0	1.3

Difference = mu (0) − mu (1)
Estimate for difference: −24.62
95% CI for difference: (−27.23, −22.01)
T-Test of difference = 0 (vs not =): T-Value = −18.79 P-Value = 0.000 DF = 76

Figure 6.26   Zero inventory items analysis.

15 minutes. Simone Fillbert noted that the data was not normal. Anita gave the advice to plot the data from each store separately, since they each represented a separate population.

Now it was time for the team to use all of the information they had discovered during the Analyze phase to make process improvements. The focus of the next phase, Improve, would be critical to getting the necessary gains to meet the corporate objectives.

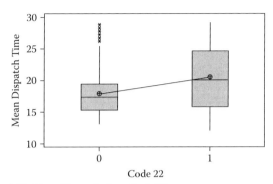

Two-Sample T-Test and CI: Mean Dispatch time, Code 22

Two-sample Test for Mean Dispatch time

Code 22	N	Mean	StdDev	SE Mean
0	292	17.93	3.35	0.20
1	73	20.49	5.16	0.60

Difference = mu (0) − mu (1)
Estimate for difference: −2.566
95% CI for difference: (−3.827, −1.304)
T-Test of difference = 0 (vs not =): T-Value = −4.04 P-Value = 0.000 DF = 87

Figure 6.27   Mean dispatch time analysis.

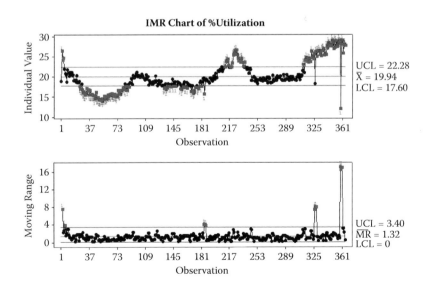

Figure 6.28   I-MR chart of %trailer utilization.

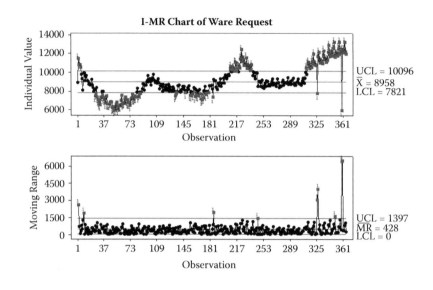

Figure 6.29   I-MR chart of warehouse requests.

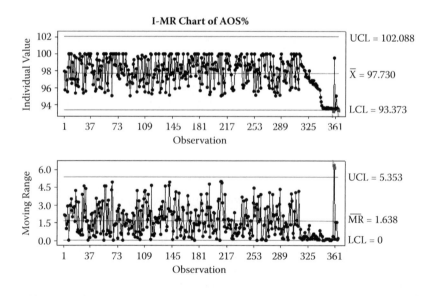

Figure 6.30   I-MR chart of AOS%.

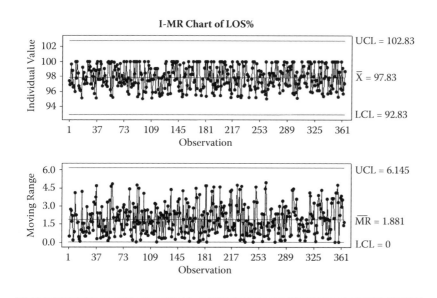

Figure 6.31   I-MR chart of LOS%.

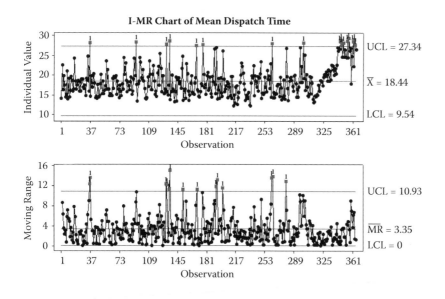

Figure 6.32   I-MR chart of mean dispatch time.

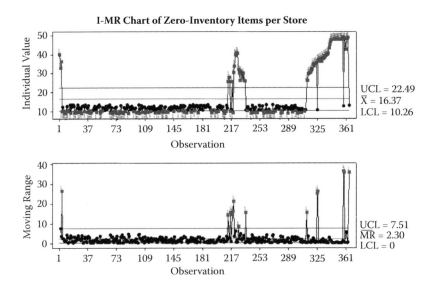

Figure 6.33   I-MR chart of zero inventory items.

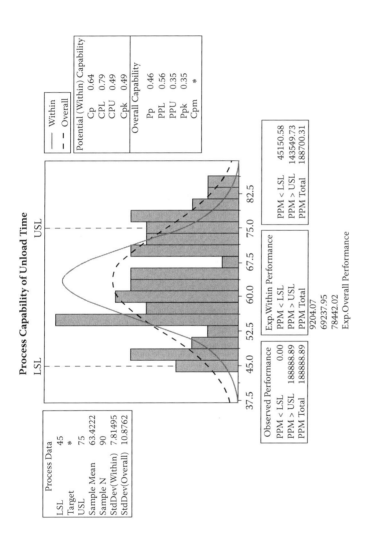

Figure 6.34   Process capability of unload time.

Chapter 7

Improve Phase

Introduction

The Define phase stated the problem; the Measure phase established a baseline; and the Analyze phase bore a root cause. Now the team needed to be creative with ways to improve %trailer utilization without changing the current customer satisfaction level. Knowing that the main root cause, warehouse demand, could not be altered, the solutions would need to be very creative. Here in the Improve phase, the solutions should be chosen to address the root cause, and they should be tested to ensure that they truly do solve the problem. Without missing a beat, Anita supplied the team with questions for Improve at their first meeting of the phase.

- What is the work breakdown structure for this project?
- What specific activities are necessary to meet the project's goals?
- How will we reintegrate the various subprojects?
- Do the changes produce the desired effects?
- Are there any unanticipated consequences?

Improve Activities	Deliverables
Identify Breakthrough and Select Practical Approaches	Improvement Recommendations
	Action (Pilot) Plans
Perform Cost/Benefit Analysis	Cost/Benefit Analysis
Design Future State	Future State Process Maps
Establish Performance Targets and Project Scorecard	Dashboards and Scorecards
Gain Approval to Implement	Recommendation Report
Train and Execute	Training Plan

Figure 7.1   Improve phase activities and deliverables.

Understanding the importance of their discussion, the team focused on the important issues and quickly divided into groups relative to the activities planned (Figure 7.1).

Identify Breakthrough and Select Practical Approaches

Finding the optimal solution was not as easy as some members had thought. The team agreed that the best solution would be to uncouple %trailer utilization from any input, so that it would be insensitive to any variation found in the inputs. Warehouse requests and trailer count currently drive the %trailer utilization value. The team brainstormed on how to better control warehouse requests and trailer count. The cause-and-effect diagram on %trailer utilization (Figure 7.2) helped drive further discussion and brainstorming.

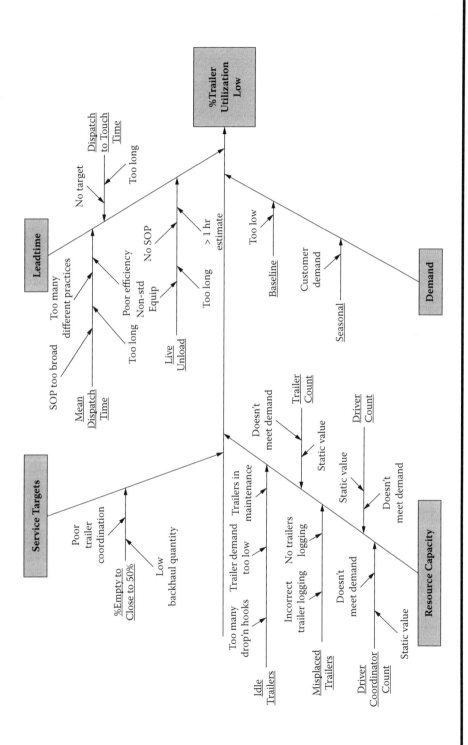

Figure 7.2 Cause-and-effect diagram for low %trailer utilization.

1) Reduce trailer and driver overhead

    a) Establish base trailer and drive count

    b) Outsource when demand is needed

2) Reduce idle time

    a) Reduce dispatch time

    b) Reduce dispatch to touch time

    c) Re-evaluate PM schedule and reduce

    d) Control live unload time (60 +/– 15 min)

3) Implement 8 wastes suggestions

4) Implement 5S process

5) Formalize and train SOPs

    a) For all critical steps

    b) Establish a training log and SOP control process

Figure 7.3 Recommendations for improvement.

After a few brainstorming sessions, it became clear that holding a static count on trailers might not be a good practice when demand is low. This became the strongest theme for their recommendations. The team also agreed, at a minimum, to recommend the improvements based on the 8 wastes and 5S analyses. The recommendations were then recorded in a table for future reference, as shown in Figure 7.3.

Action (Pilot) Plan

Based on these recommendations, the team built an action plan to perform a pilot implementation to gain process feedback. The plan included scope, new metric targets,

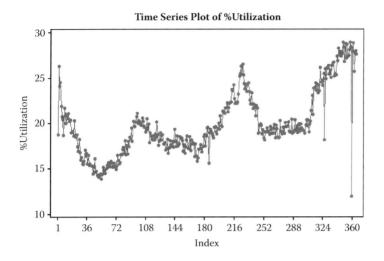

Figure 7.4   Time series plot of %trailer utilization.

stakeholders, and a communication plan. The plan involved one distribution center for the pilot study over the course of one month (April). The team selected April as the month to focus on using a time-series plot of %utilization, as shown in Figure 7.4. The goals were to reduce trailer levels (count) by 30%. At this point, it was just a plan waiting for approval.

Perform Cost/Benefit Analysis

Based on their recommendations, the team needed to financially justify the relationship between the costs of the proposed improvements versus the benefits gained. The team contacted finance and purchasing to request resources from each to perform the cost/benefit analysis. The team needed to gather the initial expected costs (Figure 7.5) to implement their recommendations. Further work was needed to estimate the savings gained relative

Recommendation	Details	Initial Cost ($millions)
30% Reduction of Trailers	Trailer net Loss or Gain	$44.45
Reduce Dispatch Time	Implement 5S	$0.06
Control Live Unload Time	New equipment Implement 5S	$15.00
Formalize and Train SOPs	Training materials Training wages Implement log and control system	$22.00
		$81.51

Figure 7.5 Expected initial costs summary.

to their recommendations (Figure 7.6). The estimates were based on the previous year's shipment data and the assumption of a 30% reduction of the trailer count. The team then built cash-flow diagrams and figured the net present worth (NPW) for their recommendations, based on the company's rate of return of 12% (compounded monthly), to show the future benefit based on a purchase made today. This is shown in Figure 7.7 with the calculations shown in Figure 7.8.

Design Future State

One of the recommendations was that the team apply the 8-wastes results to the trailer utilization process. Since there were no other major changes to the process, the only updates to the baseline process maps were the integration of the changes suggested based on the 8-wastes analysis. The process maps that were impacted included

Month	Past Daily Cost ($millions)	Projected Daily Cost ($millions)	Savings ($millions)
January	$263.19	$217.53	$45.66
February	$188.53	$133.67	$54.86
March	$219.00	$155.70	$63.30
April	$252.76	$196.30	$56.46
May	$242.00	$172.05	$69.95
June	$225.68	$160.03	$65.64
July	$271.19	$225.78	$45.41
August	$312.15	$318.70	$(6.54)
September	$250.47	$188.52	$61.94
October	$261.94	$201.74	$60.20
November	$307.20	$321.44	$(14.24)
December	$355.91	$438.14	$(82.23)

Figure 7.6 Projected monthly savings from 30% reduction in trailer count.

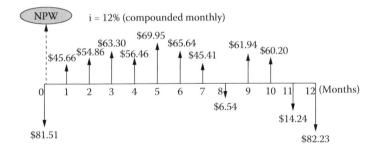

Figure 7.7 Cost/benefit analysis.

trailer request (vendor, warehouse, driver, and depot), dispatch plan maintenance (driver coordination), and trailer transport (depot–warehouse–depot). The process maps with suggested recommendations are given in Figures 7.9–7.13 with the changes highlighed.

NPW(12%) = –81.51+45.66(*P/F*, 1%, 1)+54.86(*P/F*, 1%, 2)

+63.30(*P/F*, 1%, 3)+56.46(*P/F,* 1%, 4)+69.95(*P/F,* 1%, 5)

+65.64(*P/F*, 1%, 6)+45.41(*P/F*, 1%, 7)–6.54(*P/F*, 1%, 8)

+61.94(*P/F*, 1%, 9)+60.20(*P/F*, 1%, 10)–14.24(*P/F*, 1%, 11)

–82.23(*P/F*, 1%,12)

NPW(12%) = $323.27

Figure 7.8   Cost/benefit analysis calculations.

Establish Performance Targets and Project Scorecard

With the help of the process sponsor, Robert Quincy, the team worked together to create dashboards for all stakeholders. The data for these dashboards were suggested to be automated via queries from the relative databases. The queries would update at midnight every day. The goal was to provide process information to all stakeholders in real time, not at a weekly or monthly meeting. The team decided to use daily updates due to the limitations posed by the current database. The metrics for the dashboard are given in Figure 7.14.

Scorecards were then developed based on the questions from the survey, as shown in Figure 7.15. Because the information on the survey was recalled from a month or several months prior, the team was not confident of its validity. So, the scorecards were to be distributed to the stakeholders who participated in the VOC survey. The frequency of gathering these scorecards was decided to be monthly. A designated person would then enter the data into a database to tabulate the data.

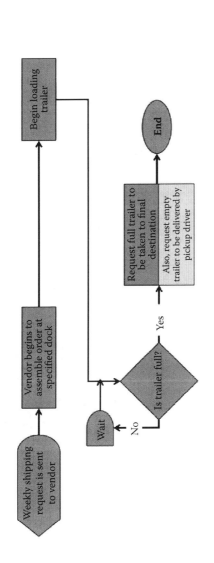

Figure 7.9   Updated process map for trailer request by vendor.

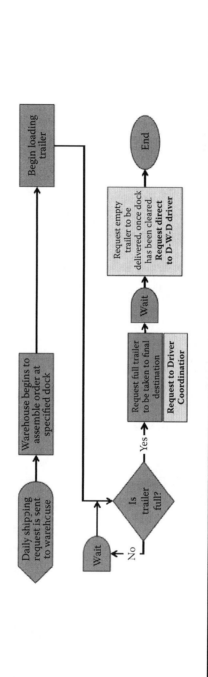

Figure 7.10   Updated process map for trailer request by warehouse.

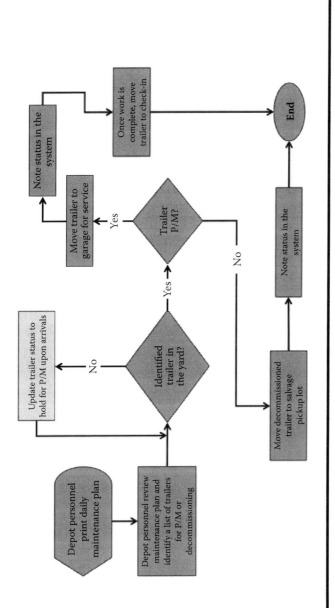

Figure 7.11   Updated process map for trailer request by depot.

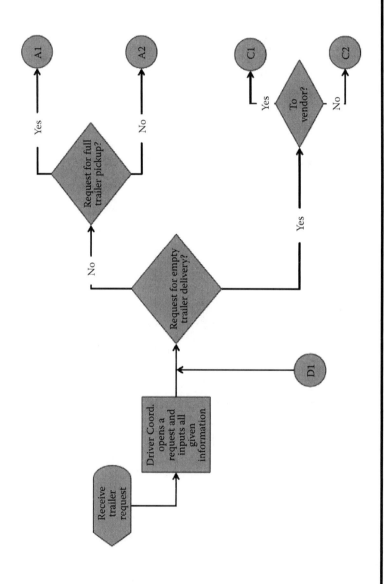

Figure 7.12 Updated process map for dispatch plan maintenance.

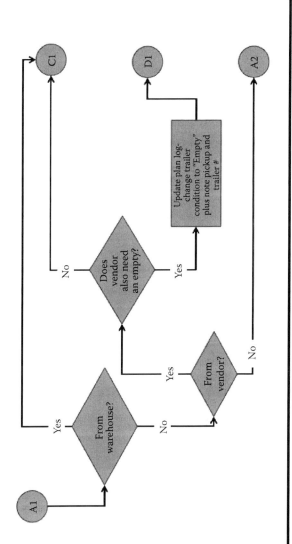

Figure 7.12 (continued).

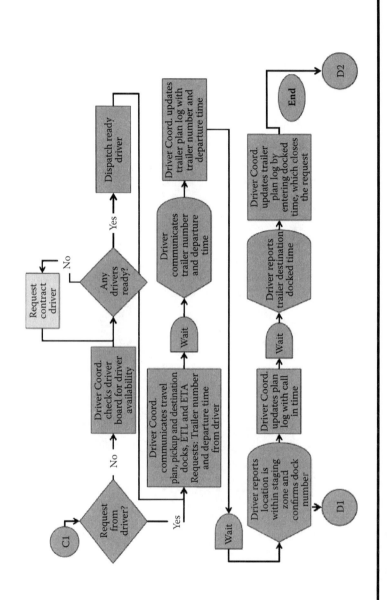

Figure 7.12 (continued).

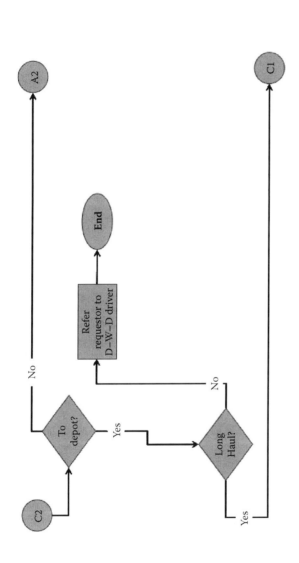

Figure 7.12 (continued).

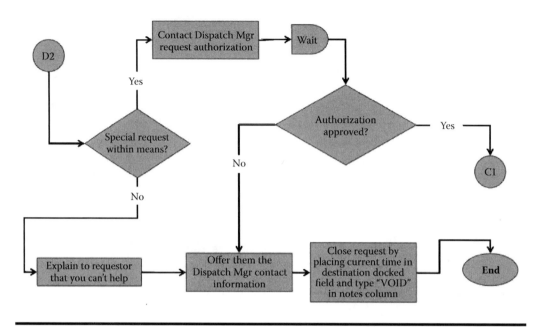

Figure 7.12 (continued).

Gain Approval to Implement, Then Implement

At this point in time, the team needed to gain approval to proceed with a pilot plan. Anita and Jim presented the current work and recommendations to the VP of transportation and the VP of distribution for the Midwest region.

Train and Execute

Once approval for the pilot was given, the team put together a training plan to go along with the pilot plan that had been created earlier. Similar to the communication RASICs, the training action plan documented who

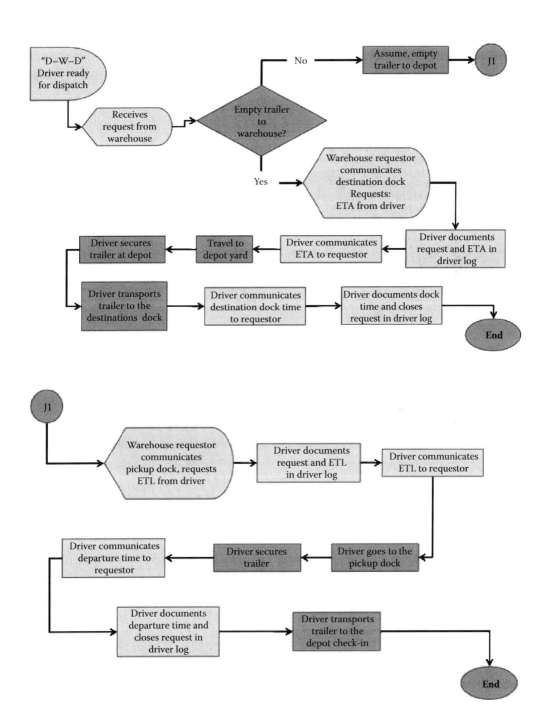

Figure 7.13 Updated process map for trailer D–W–D.

CTS	Factors	Operational Definition	Metric	Target
Realistic process time estimates and expectations	• Best practice • Equipment • Load type	Total time to unload a trailer at a store. Three fully loaded trailers will be delivered to 10 stores where the trailers will be unloaded 3 different times. A stop watch will start when the door is opened by the driver and will stop when the trailer has been emptied.	Live Unload Process Time	60 minutes
Optimized trailer dispatch plan	• Daily shipments • Trailer total available	Calculated percentage of total trailer hours used per day by total trailer hours available per day. The data source is the Trailer Plan Log.	%Trailer Utilization	30%
Meet store customers' demands	• Unpredicted demand change • Vendor supply	Daily total of merchandise that is at a zero quantity divided by the total number of stores. The data source is from all stores' inventory at midnight each day.	Zero Inventory Items per Store	5 items
Optimized trailer dispatch plan	• Route estimate (ETA) • LOS% • Timing of the driver's call and the logging	Calculated percentage of shipments that arrive on time by total shipments per day. The data source is the Trailer Plan Log, which, when queried will produce the total daily shipments and the total late AOS shipments by day(AOS has no tolerance, ETA is goal). 1-(late shipments/total) will produce the AOS%.	AOS%	100%

Figure 7.14   VOP matrix-metrics for the dashboard.

CTS	Factors	Operational Definition	Metric	Target
Optimized trailer dispatch plan	• Driver coordinator's decision	Calculated percentage of shipments that leave on time by total shipments per day. The data source is the Trailer Plan Log, which, when queried will produce the total daily shipments and the total late LOS shipments by day (LOS has no tolerance. ETL is goal). 1-(late shipments/ total) will produce the LOS%.	LOS%	100%
	• Driver availability • Coordinator's work load	Calculated average of dispatch time in minutes by day. The data source is the Trailer Plan Log, which, when queried will produce the dispatch time (Dispatch time – Request time) which will then be averaged by day.	Dispatch Mean	15 minutes

Figure 7.14   (continued).

was receiving training, what type of training they would receive, and by whom they were to be trained, as shown in Figures 7.16 and 7.17. The team kept this plan as orderly and updated as possible, since they anticipated using the same plan for the entire region.

CTS	Factors	Operational Definition	Metric	Target
Open communication of critical or jeopardy events		Transportation: Driver Coord. Q1 "Within the last month, how often did drivers show up late at the destination dock without calling to alert you before their arrival?" Q2 "Within the last month, how often did you notify a requestor of a late delivery or pickup before the trailer made it to the dock?" Drivers: Q3 "Within the last month, how often did you show up late at the destination dock without calling to alert a driver coordinator before your arrival?" Q4 "Within the last month, how many times have you called a business critical resource and could not make contact within 1 hour?" Store Personnel: Store Mgrs., Rec. Dock Q5 "Within the last month, how often did a trailer show up late at the destination dock without anybody calling to alert you before its arrival?" Q6 "Within the last month, how many times were you placed on hold waiting for a driver coordinator?"	% responded by question	Q1 100% Never Q2 100% Never Q3 100% Never Late Q4 100% Never Q5 100% Never Late Q6 100% Never

Figure 7.15

CTS	Factors	Operational Definition	Metric	Target
Open communication of critical or jeopardy events		Vendor: Op Mgrs., Shipping Dock Q7 "Within the last month, how often did a trailer show up late at the destination dock without anybody calling to alert you before its arrival?" Q8 "Within the last month, how many times were you placed on hold waiting for a driver coordinator?" Warehouse: Mgrs., Shipping & Rec. Dock Q9 "Within the last month, how often did a trailer show up late at the destination dock without anybody calling to alert you before its arrival?" Q10 "Within the last month, how many times were you placed on hold waiting for a driver coordinator?"	% responded by question	Q7 100% Never Late Q8 100% Never Q9 100% Never Late Q10 100% Never
Up-to-date trailer status	Incorrect logging of trailer	Calculated percentage of the incorrect trailer status tally by the total trailers audited. Trailer status data is extracted from Trailer Plan Log in real-time during the audit. A random list of 5% of the trailers will be used to choose the trailers to audit.	Trailer Status Error Rate	0%

Figure 7.15 (continued).

CTS	Factors	Operational Definition	Metric	Target
Documented standard process	• Defined need • Resources not available	Percentage of formal SOPs in place by total SOPs possible. SOP audit of processes outlined by Six Sigma team relative to the process maps built for the Measure phase. Check-sheet method used to tally if a formal SOP was published and distributed to those affected.	Existing SOP%	100%
	• Weak training • No training log • No audit	Percentage of the number of positive responses (yes) relative to survey question by total responses. The survey question will be presented to the stakeholder groups. Percent responded will be calculated overall and broken down by rating group "Do you know the (CJ-Mart) operating procedures that affect you?"	Knowledge of Existing SOP%	100% yes

Figure 7.15   (continued).

Responsible (R) Approval (A) Support (S) Inform (I) Consult (C)	Project Leader Anita Smith	Process Owner Robert Quincy	Project Champion Thompson	CI Mentor/MBB Jim Pulls	Finance Joe Thompson	Team Member 1 Paul Jones	Team Member 2 Dave Leader	Team Member 3 Simone Fillbert	Team Member 4 Cindy Patch	Team Member 5 Chris Roberts	Team Member 6 Mike O'Conner
Training Plan	R	S	A	I		S	S	S	S	S	S
Training Materials	R	A	S	I							
Drivers	S					R	S				S
Transportation	S						R	S			S
Warehouse	S							R	S		S
Store	S								R	S	S
Vendor	S									R	S
Training Schedule	R	S	A	I	S	S	S	S	S	S	S
Driver Training Leader	S					R	S				S
Transportation Training Leader	S						R	S			S
Warehouse Training Leader	S							R	S		S
Store Training Leader	S								R	S	S
Vendor Training Leader	S									R	S
Pilot Support Plan	R	A	S	C		B	S	S	S	S	S

Figure 7.16   Training action plan RASIC.

Level of Participation Invited (X)	Transportation General Mgrs.	Transportation Dispatch Mgrs.	Transportation Driver Coord.	Driver	Warehouse General Mgrs.	Warehouse Rec. Mgrs.	Warehouse Shipping Mgrs.	Warehouse Dock Personnel	Vendor Operations Mgr.	Vendor Shipping Mgr.	Vendor Dock Personnel	Store General Mgrs.	Store Rec. Personnel
Pilot Overview	X	X	X	X	X	X	X	X	X	X	X	X	X
Transpo-1	X	X	X										
Transpo-2			X										
Drivers				X									
Warehouse-1					X	X	X	X					
Warehouse-2								X					
Vendor									X	X	X		
Store-1												X	X
Store-2													X

Figure 7.17 Training action matrix of course offerings.

Chapter 8

Control Phase

Introduction

Here in the Control phase, the team was to focus on how to maintain the improvements that were seen in the data from the execution of the pilot plan. Their goal was to ensure that the key variables remain within the acceptable ranges under the modified process. Jim Pulls suggested that the controls might be as simple as using checklists or periodic status reviews to ensure that proper procedures were followed, or they could be as detailed as using process control charts to monitor the performance of key measures. No matter, Anita started the phase as she always did, with a list of questions for the team to discuss at the first meeting of the phase.

- During the project, how will we control risk, quality, cost, schedule, scope, and changes to the plan?
- What types of progress reports should we send to sponsors?
- How will we ensure that the business goals of the project are accomplished?
- How will we maintain the gains made?

Control Activities	Deliverables
Measure Results and Manage Change	1) Hypothesis Test
Report Scorecard Data and Create Process Control Plan	2) Mistake Proofing
	3) FMEA and Control Plan
	4) Process Capability (DPMO)
Apply PDCA Process	5) Statistical Process Control (SPC)
Identify Replication Opportunities	6) Standard Work
Develop Future Plans	7) Lessons Learned

Figure 8.1   Control phase activities and deliverables.

As a result of the phase's kickoff meeting, the team compiled their list of activities and deliverables associated with those activities, as seen in Figure 8.1. The first hurdle was the hypothesis test, which was used to judge the pilot data results.

Measure Results and Manage Change

After the pilot, the team needed to confirm that the changes made to the process had impacted the output of the process. So, the team used the hypothesis test to check for a difference between the mean %trailer utilization before the pilot and after the pilot, as shown in Figure 8.2 (Data Figure 8.2). They also wanted to confirm that there was not a change in customer satisfaction via the AOS% (arrive on schedule), as shown in Figure 8.3. The results were favorable, which allowed the team to continue. If the results were not favorable, the team would have had to choose between running the pilot

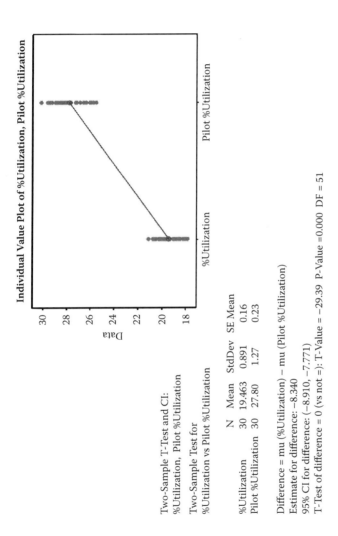

Individual Value Plot of %Utilization, Pilot %Utilization

Two-Sample T-Test and CI:
%Utilization, Pilot %Utilization
Two-Sample Test for
%Utilization vs Pilot %Utilization

	N	Mean	StdDev	SE Mean
%Utilization	30	19.463	0.891	0.16
Pilot %Utilization	30	27.80	1.27	0.23

Difference = mu (%Utilization) − mu (Pilot %Utilization)
Estimate for difference: −8.340
95% CI for difference: (−8.910, −7.771)
T-Test of difference = 0 (vs not =): T-Value = −29.39 P-Value =0.000 DF = 51

Figure 8.2 %trailer utilizaiton analysis.

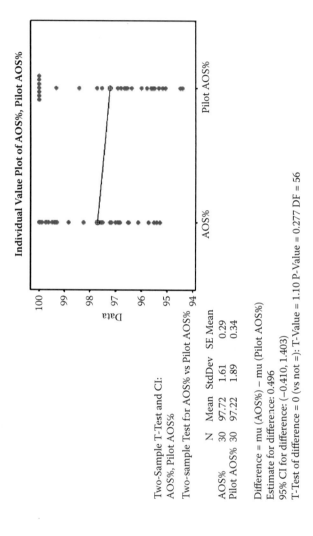

Figure 8.3   AOS% analysis.

longer to collect more data, or offering new recommendations and running a new pilot.

Report Scorecard Data and Create Process Control Plan

Dave Leader stepped up as the mistake-proof expert for the team. He had prior Lean training on this concept, which allowed the team to excel here. They reviewed each step of the process and referenced the cause-and-effect diagrams and why–why diagrams, looking for failures for which they could plan to prevent or mitigate the risk. Figure 8.4 is an example of a new diagram that allowed the team to identify root causes in the trailer plan log.

For example, instead of allowing the driver coordinator a chance for error, they requested that the software not allow blanks. The team found that they needed a few more cause-and-effect diagrams to pull out some more areas of improvement. Using the cause-and-effect diagrams, action plans were created to highlight the possible areas for mistakes and identify methods of correction, as shown in Figure 8.5.

FMEA and Control Plan

The team revisited the Failure Mode and Effects Analysis (FMEA) that was started in the Analyze phase, as shown in Figure 8.6. The live-unload process and the dispatch process had been changed due to the recommendations, and many of the failure modes reduced. So the team

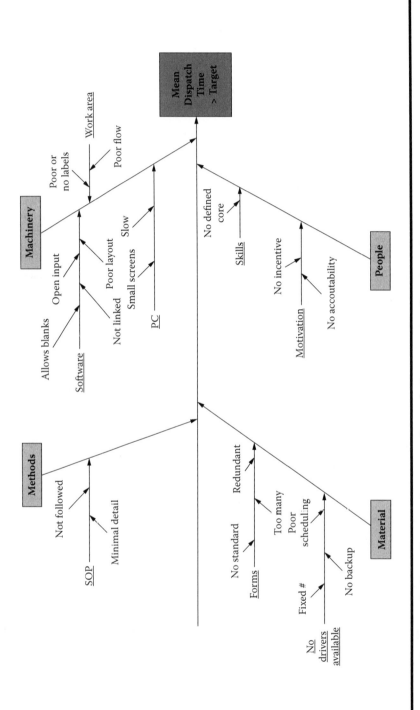

Figure 8.4   Cause-and-effect diagram for mean dispatch time greater than target.

Process	Location	Mistake	Fix
Dispatch Plan Maintenance	Trailer Plan Log Database	Missing data	Do not allow blanks
		Incorrect driver	Pre-populated list of drivers pulled from Driver Status Database: only ready or empty status
		Missed backhaul	Pre-populated driver list shows departure and destination

Figure 8.5   Mistake proofing.

reevaluated the processes and established a control plan based on these new figures, as shown in Figure 8.7. The defined target for the live-unload process became 60 ± 15 minutes, and the target for the dispatch process became 15 ± 5 minutes, which is provided in the control plan (Figure 8.8).

Process Capability/DPMO

Previously, only the live-unload time was designated as having a target and tolerance that would be a good candidate for capability reporting. However, a standard audit was put in place to measure the effectiveness of the driver coordinator. Here, the defects per million opportunities (DPMO) were the mistakes that a coordinator might make while updating the trailer plan log. This is similar to the data collected for the gauge R&R (repeatability and reproducibility) study. To calculate the DPMO for the trailer plan update process, the audit documented

Process Function	Potential Failure Mode	Potential Effects of Failure	S E V — How severe is the effect to the customer?	Potential Cause(s)/ Mechanism(s) of Failure	O C C — Hoe often does the cause of failure mode occur?	Current Process Controls	D E T — How well can you detect cause or FM?	R P N — SEV x OCC x DET
The highest value process steps from the C&E matrix.	In what ways might the process potentially fail to meet the requirements and or design intent?	What is the effect of each failure mode on the outputs and/or customer requirements? The customer could be the next operation, subsequent operations, another division, or the end user.		How can the failure occur? Describe in terms of something that can be corrected or controlled. Be specific. Try to identify the causes that directly impact the failure mode, i.e., root causes.		What are the existing controls and procedures (inspection and test) that either prevent the failure mode from occurring or detect the failure should it occur? **Should include an SOP number.**		
Live Unload Process	Last too long	Miss scheduled departure time	3	No best practice used; improper equipment used; no room to put unloaded product	10	none	10	300
Dispatch Process	Incorrect logging of request information	Delayed pickup or delivery of trailer	6	Incorrect request input; illegible request input; typo	4	none	10	240
	Last too long	Delayed pickup or delivery of trailer	6	No driver available; workload too large; poor organization	6	none	10	360

Figure 8.6   Failure modes and effects analysis.

Process Function	Potential Failure Mode	Potential Effects of Failure	Recommended Action(s)	Responsibility and Completion Date	Actions Taken	Action Result			
						What are the new severity? (S E V)	What is the new process capability? (O C C)	Are the detection limits improved? (D E T)	Recoankpute RPN after actions are complete (R P N)
The highest value process steps from the C&E matrix	In what ways might the process potentially fail to meet the process requirements and or design intent?	What is the effect of each failure mode on the outputs and/or customer requirements? The custumer could be the next operation, another division, or the end user.	What are the actions for reducing the occurrence or improving detection, or for identifying the root cause if it is unknown? **Should have action only on high RPNs or easy fixes.**	Who is responsible for the recommended action?	List the completed actions that are recalculated RPN, Include the implementation date for any changes.				
Live Unload Process	Last too long	Miss scheduled departure time	Define best practices that reduce equipment list specifications	Store and Lean Six Sigma team	Implemented 5S, standard work, and dashboard for Live Unload Time	3	5	1	15
Dispatch Process	Incorrect logging of request infomation	Delayed pickup or trailer	Define a best practice that instructs how to make a request and control input with a standard form. Implement a confirmation process.	Transportation and Lean Six Sigma team	Implemented 5S, standard work, and dashboard for Mean Dispatch Time	6	5	1	30
	Last too long	Delayed pickup or delivery of trailer	Use 5S and 8Wastes to anlayze the process and create a list of recommendations	Transportaion and Lean Six Sigma Team	Implemented 5S, standard work, and dashboard for Mean Dispatch Time	6	5	1	30

Figure 8.7   FMEA after implementing corrective actions.

Process	Live Unload	Dispatch of Trailers
What's Controlled	Unloading Time	Dispatch Time
Input or Output	Input (to total trailer time)	Input (to total trailer time)
Spec Limits	60 +/–15 min	15 +/–5 min
Measurement Method	Logging from Trailer Plan Database	Logging from Trailer Plan Database
Sample Size	5	2
Frequency	Daily	Hourly
Who/What Measures	Driver calls in docked time and departure time to Coordinator who logs event	Coordinator inputs request time and then dispatch time
Where Recorded	Transpo Process Website	Transpo Process Website
SOP	Driver Long Haul and Dispatch Plan Maintenance	Dispatch Plan Maintenance

Figure 8.8   Control plan.

the total number of opportunities for errors and the total number of errors. DPMO was calculated as follows:

$$\mathrm{DPMO} = \frac{\text{Defects Discovered}}{\text{Total Opportunities}} \times 1,000,000$$

Now, for the live-unload time, the capability is calculated and graphed as shown in Figure 8.9 (Data Figure 8.9).

Apply P-D-C-A Process

The team decided to track a select few metrics with statistical process control (SPC) to monitor the process and be alerted before trouble strikes. For example, one metric

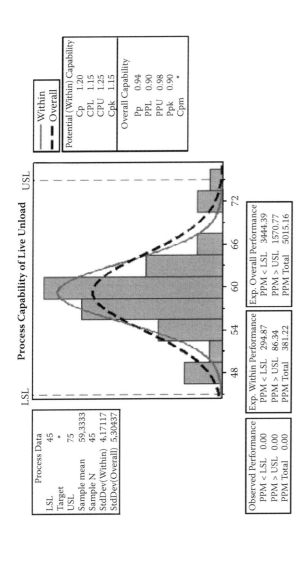

Figure 8.9 Process capability for live unload.

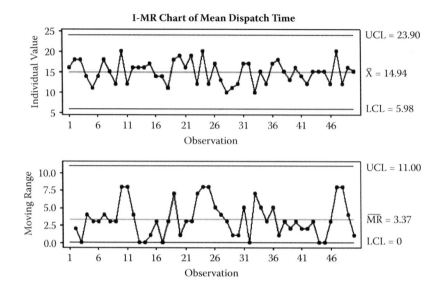

Figure 8.10   I-MR chart for mean dispatch time.

that would be tracked was the mean dispatch time, as shown in Figure 8.10 (Data Figure 8.10). Every hour, two dispatch events are recorded and plotted. This run chart will identify when the driver coordinators become overloaded. In addition, the team created a control chart for live-unload times, as shown in Figure 8.11 (Data Figure 8.11). The team thought that these were good indicators for management to look into the problem.

Identify Replication Opportunities

Standard work was the Lean tool that helped the team document the live-unload process so that each store could repeat it with minimal variability in process time. Live-unload time was noted as idle time; therefore, the

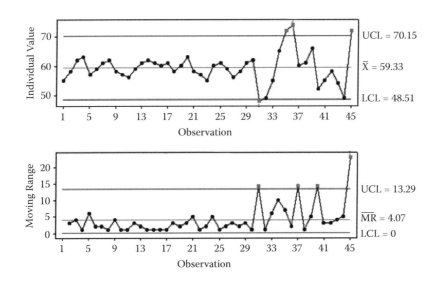

Figure 8.11   I-MR chart for live unload time.

team needed to minimize it and control its variation to reduce waste and control cost. The team that led the gauge R&Rs worked with the three stores that were measured. A best practice was agreed to, and then the team performed a standard work exercise to document the process from driver arriving at the dock to driver leaving the dock. The team started by calculating the takt time based on customer requirements, as shown in Figure 8.12.

The store dock personnel typically unload seven trucks within an 8-hour shift. The store has three docks with three staging aisles to allow for product check-in, as shown in Figure 8.12. Each truck is unloaded by means of a standard forklift, and each truck has 20 pallets that must be removed one at a time. The steps for the process of unloading the truck are documented in Figure 8.12.

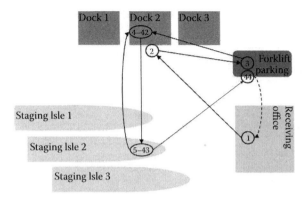

Figure 8.12   Standard work sheet.

Develop Future Plans

Now that the team had completed the project and had found success, they prepared to close out the work. Robert Quincy agreed to support the new process changes for the Midwest region, because he was the process sponsor. The team had done a great job of documenting the new procedures, control documents, and training programs. So, all that was left was to meet to discuss lessons learned during the project. Many members had input about the tools used and the effectiveness of each. Jim Pulls reminded the group that, typically, not all tools are used for a Lean Six Sigma project, because some tools overlap and others were designed for particular applications. In this project, the team not only completed a Lean Six Sigma project, but they had also generated a case study that will be used to train other company employees. With that said, Jim tasked the team to use a few extra tools with the idea that the results were to be used for educational purposes. Jim Pulls congratulated the team for completing two jobs at once! Then he stopped and calmly asked Anita to continue with the lessons learned.

Chapter 9

Conclusions

Lean Six Sigma is a methodology whose use is growing throughout all industries. Lean is a powerful methodology utilized to reduce wastes in processes, thus reducing lead time and costs. Six Sigma is a also a powerful methodology strongly rooted in statistical techniques used to reduce variation in processes. Organizations can reap gains from each method. However, it is the integration of the two methodologies as Lean Six Sigma that provides a more dramatic impact to the organizational culture and the bottom line.

When implementing Lean Six Sigma, significant training is needed to ensure that the team is fully knowledgeable and has the necessary resources. However, due to time restrictions and the need to manage Lean Six Sigma projects, it is useful to develop fully supportive case studies to facilitate the instruction. Case studies can be used either throughout the training to further reinforce concepts or as conceptual overviews. This book provides a case study from start to finish to illustrate the combined Lean Six Sigma methodology.

Lean Six Sigma Glossary

5S: A method of creating a self-sustaining culture that perpetuates an organized, clean, and efficient work place. Also referred to as the five pillars of the visual workplace.

8 wastes: See *waste*.

affinity diagram: A tool to organize ideas and data which allows a large number of ideas to be sorted into groups.

Analyze phase: Third step of the Six Sigma Define–Measure–Analyze–Improve–Control phase. Data is analyzed in this step to verify cause-and-effect relationships and determine the relationships.

appraisal cost: A cost of poor quality associated with, but not limited to, test and inspection, supplier acceptance sampling, and auditing processes.

attribute gauge R&R: Measurement systems analysis performed on qualitative data in an effort to gauge repeatability and reproducibility.

audit: A method of assessing the effectiveness of process improvement.

baseline: The starting point of a current process with respect to process metrics.

benchmarking: An activity to establish internal expectations for excellence, based on direct comparison to "best." In some cases, the best is not a direct competitor in your industry.

Black Belt: A person trained to execute critical projects for breakthrough improvements to enhance the bottom line.

boundary: The starting and stopping point of a process under consideration for process improvements.

box plot: A method of graphically depicting groups of numerical data through five-number summaries.

brainstorming: A technique to generate a large number of ideas in a short period of time.

breakthrough thinking: A method of brainstorming for creative problem solving that promotes unique, out-of-the-box thinking.

business case: A written document that provides the reasoning for initiating a project or task.

capability: The ability of a process to meet customer specifications.

capacity: The ability to meet production requirements.

cause-and-effect diagram: A diagram that shows the causes of a specific event. The purpose is to identify potential factors that cause an overall effect. Also known as the Ishikawa diagram or fishbone diagram.

check sheets: A document used for collecting data in real time. This document should be designed for efficient recording of data.

communication/influence strategy: A matrix developed based on the customer/stakeholders matrix to ensure that the proper audience is provided the right information at the right time, as identified in the communications plan.

communications plan: A guide to communicating the right information at the right time to the right audience in an appropriate format/medium.

control chart: A tool used to determine if a process is in a state of statistical control. Also known as the Shewhart chart.

Control phase: Fifth step of the Six Sigma Define–Measure–Analyze–Improve–Control phase. In this step, control mechanisms are implemented and the process is monitored.

control plan: A method of controlling product characteristics and their associated process variables to ensure capability of the process/product over time.

core team: Typically a cross-functional team responsible for completing a project successfully.

correlation analysis: A statistical method that indicates the strength and direction of a linear relationship between two random variables.

cost/benefit analysis: A process to assess the business case for a project. The total expected costs are weighted against the total expected benefits to choose the most profitable option.

cost of poor quality (COPQ): Costs associated with not doing things right the first time. Examples of COPQ include scrap, rework, and waste.

critical to quality (CTQ): Key measurable product or service characteristics defined by the customer.

critical to satisfaction (CTS): Key measurable product or service characteristics necessary to satisfy customer requirements. Often referred to as *critical to quality*.

current state: The current steps, delays, and information flows necessary to deliver a product or service.

customer: Anyone who uses or consumes a product or service. A customer can be internal or external to the provider.

customer-needs map (CNM): A matrix of customer needs that is decomposed into more detailed and focused matrices to ensure that all customer needs are adequately addressed.

customers/stakeholders matrix: A matrix that consists of different stakeholders and their needs/requirements along one axis. Each need/requirement is weighted according to relative importance and then translated into technical requirements.

data collection plan: The process of preparing and collecting data for process improvement.

defect: A nonconformance in a product or service.

defects per million opportunities (DPMO): A measure of process performance in opportunities per million units.

Define phase: First step of the Six Sigma Define–Measure–Analyze–Improve–Control phase. This step defines the high-level project goals and the current process.

deliverable: A tangible or intangible object resulting from a project task.

deviation: The difference between an observed value and the mean of all observed values.

DMAIC process: The Six Sigma Define–Measure–Analyze–Improve–Control process.

failure cost: The cost of poor quality (COPQ) associated with internal and external failures. Internal failure costs are incurred from rework and scrap. External failure costs are those costs related to defective parts that are shipped to the customer.

failure mode and effects analysis (FMEA): A structured approach to assess the magnitude of potential failures and identify the sources of each potential failure. Corrective actions are then identified and implemented to prevent failure occurrence.

flexibility: The ability to respond to changes in demand, customer requirements, etc.

future state: The ideal process steps and information flows for delivering a product or service.

gauge repeatability and reproducibility (gauge R&R): A method of collecting data to assess the variation in the measurement system and compare it to the total process variation.

Green Belt: An individual trained to assist a Black Belt. This individual may also undertake projects of a lesser scope than Black Belt projects.

ground rules: Procedures and limits agreed to by a team for conducting a meeting or handling a project.

histogram: A graphical tool that shows frequencies of data as bars.

hypothesis: A proposed explanation put forward usually to test using the scientific method.

hypothesis test: A method to make statistical decisions using experimental data.

Improve phase: Fourth step of the Six Sigma Define–Measure–Analyze–Improve–Control phase. In this step, the process is optimized based on the data analyses from the Analyze phase.

input: A resource that is consumed, utilized, or added during a process.

intangible cost: Costs that are difficult to measure because they are not monetary.

items for resolution (ITR): A list of action items to complete a project or phase of a project.

lead time: The total time required to deliver an order to the customer.

Lean: A process-management philosophy that focuses on the reduction of non-value-added activities or wastes.

Lean Six Sigma: An integrated methodology that combines Six Sigma and Lean using the DMAIC (Define–Measure–Analyze–Improve–Control) process.

Master Black Belt: A Six Sigma expert who is responsible for the strategic implementation within an organization. This involves the training and mentoring of Black Belts and Green Belts.

mean: The sum of all data points divided by the number of data points. Often referred to as the average.

measurement system analysis: A mathematical method of calculating how much variation within a measurement process contributes to overall process variability.

Measure phase: Second step of the Six Sigma Define–Measure–Analyze–Improve–Control phase. In this step, relevant data is collected on the current process.

metric: A performance measure that is linked to the goals and objectives of an organization.

milestone timeline: A graph or chart depicting the key steps or tasks required in a project over time.

mistake proofing: A mechanism that helps avoid mistakes by preventing or correcting errors as they occur.

operating costs: Recurring expenses related to business operations or the operation of equipment or the facility.

operational definition: A description of a product or process characteristic and how to collect and measure the characteristic.

opportunity cost: A cost of poor quality (COPQ) associated with a loss in market share or to the competition due to lower product quality.

organization chart: A diagram that shows the structure and relationships within an organization.

output: A product or service delivered by a process.

Pareto diagram: A vertical bar graph for attribute or categorical data that shows the bars in descending order of significance, ordered from left to right. Helps to focus on the vital few problems rather than the trivial many. An extension of the Pareto Principle suggests that the significant items in a given group normally constitute a relatively small portion of the items in the total group. Conversely, a majority of the items will be relatively minor in significance (i.e., the 80/20 rule).

Plan–Do–Check–Act (PDCA): PDCA is a repeatable four-phase implementation strategy for process improvement. PDCA is an important item for control in policy deployment. Sometimes referred to as the Deming or PDCA cycle.

prevention cost: A cost of poor quality (COPQ) associated with stopping defects from occurring before they can happen. This is where money should be spent to reduce defects.

preventive maintenance (PM): The maintenance of equipment and facilities using systematic inspection, detection, and correction to reduce failures from occurring.

problem solving: A process of identifying a problem, using the scientific method to determine root causes, and implementing corrective actions to prevent the problem from recurring.

process: An activity that blends inputs to produce a product, provide a service, or perform a task.

process capability: A measurement of the capability of a process to meet customer specifications. Usually expressed as a process capability index such as Cp or Cpk.

process flow diagram: A pictorial representation of a process that illustrates the inputs, main steps, branches, and outcomes of a process. A problem-solving tool that illustrates a process. It can show the "as is" process or "should be" process for comparison and should make waste evident.

process input variables: A process is a blending of various inputs with a goal of achieving a specific output. Inputs to a process generally include material, people, equipment, methods/procedures, and environment.

process map: A visual representation of the sequential flow of a process. Used as a tool in problem solving, this technique makes opportunities for improvement apparent.

process output variables: A desired output of a process as specified by the customer. Outputs typically include a stated service, product, or task per customer requirements.

process sponsor/owner: The individual responsible for the design and performance of a specific process.

project champion: A business leader or senior manager who is responsible for ensuring that resources are available for the successful completion of a project.

project charter: A statement of the scope, objectives, and team members for a project. It includes the problem statement, objectives, and goals.

project goal: The desired achievement from a process improvement project.

project plan: The actions and procedures required to achieve the project goal(s).

project scope: The processes and work required to successfully complete a project.

project timeline: The chronological sequence of events necessary for completing a project.

quality characteristic: An aspect of a product or service that is vital to its ability to perform its intended function.

Quality Function Deployment (QFD): A methodology to transform the voice of the customer into product or service characteristics.

regression analysis: A tool for modeling and analyzing numerical data using a dependent or response variable and one or more independent or explanatory variables.

responsibilities matrix: A matrix that identifies each team member and their respective responsibilities to ensure successful completion of the project or of specific project phases.

Responsible Accountable Support Informed Consulted (RASIC) matrix: A matrix that describes the participation responsibility of roles for completing tasks or deliverables for a project.

risk management: The identification, assessment, prioritization, and control/minimization of project and process risks.

root cause: The ultimate reason for an event or condition.

service flowdown diagram: A graphical representation of a process depicting the various levels of the entire process as a means of identifying the key areas of service to the stakeholders.

sigma (σ): Standard deviation of a statistical population.

sigma capability: A measure of process capability that represents the number of standard deviations between the center of a process and the closest specification limit. See also *sigma level*.

sigma level: A measure of process capability that represents the number of standard deviations between the center of a process and the closest specification limit. See also *sigma capability*.

SIPOC (Suppliers, Inputs, Process, Outputs, Customers): A methodology to identify the suppliers, inputs, process, output, and customers of a process. It is a graphical representation to help identify all key stakeholders.

Six Sigma: A quality-improvement and business strategy that emphasizes impacting the bottom line by reducing defects, reducing cycle time, and reducing costs. Six Sigma began in the 1980s at Motorola.

spaghetti chart: A map that illustrates the path of a product as it travels through the value stream.

stakeholder: An individual who is affected by or who can influence a project or process.

stakeholder analysis matrix: A matrix used to identify stakeholders and gain support for developing a project action plan.

standard deviation: A measure of variability in a data set. It is the square root of the variance.

standardization: The system of documenting and updating procedures to make sure everyone knows clearly and simply what is expected of them. Essential for the application of the PDCA (Plan–Do–Check–Act) cycle.

standard operating procedure (SOP): A prescribed documented method or process that is sustainable, repeatable, and predictable.

standard work: A tool that defines the interaction of people and their environment when processing a product or service. It details the motion of the operator and the sequence of action. It provides a routine for consistency of an operation and a basis for improvement. Standard work has three central elements: takt time, standard work sequence, and standard work in process.

statistical process control (SPC): A method of process monitoring using control charts.

strategic goals: The overall goal of an organization, typically in terms of gaining market position long term.

strategy: A plan of action to achieve a specific goal.

system model map: A diagram representing the process and its respective inputs and outputs. Also known as an input–process–output (IPO) diagram.

takt time: The frequency with which the customer wants a product. How frequently a sold unit must be produced. The number is derived by dividing the available production time in a shift by the customer demand for the product. Takt time is usually expressed in seconds.

target: An objective or goal.

team member: A person linked to a team for a common goal and purpose.

technical, political, or cultural (TPC) analysis: A methodology to identify, label, and understand sources of resistance from technical, political, or cultural sources.

test for normality: A statistical process to determine if a sample or group of data fits a standard normal distribution.

time series: A sequence of data points measured at time intervals.

total productive maintenance (TPM): Productive maintenance carried out by all employees. It is based on the principle that equipment improvement must involve everyone in the organization, from line operators to top management.

utility: The amount of satisfaction obtained from the entire consumption of a product.

validation: The confirmation that customer needs are met.

value: A capability provided to a customer for an appropriate price.

value added: Any process or operation that shapes or transforms the product or service into a final form that the customer will purchase.

value stream: All activities required to design and produce a product from conception to launch, order to delivery, and raw materials to the customer.

value stream mapping: A process for identifying all activities required to produce a product or product family. This is usually represented pictorially in a value stream map.

variance: A measure of variability in a data set or population. Variance is equal to the squared value of standard deviation.

variation: A process is said to exhibit variation or variability if there are changes or differences in the process.

visual control: Visual regulation of operations, tool placement, etc., that provides a method for understanding a process at a glance.

visual management: Systems that enable anyone to immediately assess the current status of an operation or given process at a glance, regardless of their knowledge of the process.

voice of the customer (VOC): Desires and requirements of the customer at all levels, translated into real terms for consideration in the development of new products, services, and daily business conduct.

voice of the process (VOP): This is what the process is capable of achieving. It is typically depicted by plotting data using a control chart to determine if the process is under control and how much variation exists.

waste: Also known as *muda*. Any process or operation that adds cost or time and does not add value. Eight types of waste have been identified:

1. Waste from overproduction
2. Waste from waiting or idle time
3. Waste from unnecessary transportation

4. Waste from inefficient processes
5. Waste from unnecessary stock on hand
6. Waste of motion and efforts
7. Waste from producing defective goods
8. Waste from unused creativity

why–why exercise: A simple problem-solving method of analyzing a problem or issue by asking "Why" five times. The root cause should become evident by continuing to ask why a situation exists.

Index